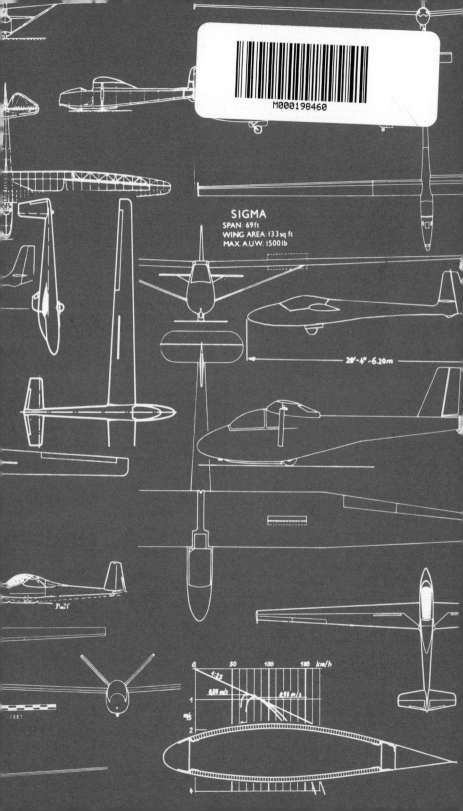

SIGMA
SPAN: 69 ft
WING AREA: 133 sq ft
MAX. A.U.W.: 1500 lb

SOARING
CROSS
COUNTRY

SOARING CROSS COUNTRY

by ED BYARS
BILL HOLBROOK

Published by SOARING SYMPOSIA
408 Washington Street
Cumberland, Maryland 21502

Manufactured in the United States of America
by LithoCrafters, Inc.,
Ann Arbor, Michigan 48106

Dedicated to . . .
  our loyal crew chiefs . . .
    Betsy and Sophie

TABLE OF CONTENTS

Page

PREFACE

This textbook evolved from extending and expanding class notes which we developed for use in our symposia on soaring cross country. It should perhaps be thought of as an intermediate text and it presumes that the reader has gone through elementary training in sailplanes and has post solo experience and is now ready to think about soaring cross country. It is also intermediate in the sense that we would expect potential readers to have already read such excellent elementary works as *The Joy of Soaring* and parts of *The American Soaring Handbook*, and after reading and studying this book they would be ready to proceed on to the more advanced texts such as the Proceedings of the Symposia on Competitive Soaring.

We have tried to make this a non-technical presentation which stresses philosophy and ideas about how to make more intelligent soaring decisions. You will not find detailed discussions on sailplane aerodynamics nor, for example, detailed explanation of such things as vortex theories of thermals, etc. We do hope, however, that after you have read this book, you will have gained appreciable confidence in your own ability to safely embark on either your first or additionally expanded cross country flights.

We think and hope this book and its contents will have significance for soaring in all parts of the world; however, we frankly admit that it is written from the American viewpoint and emphasizes the American approach, American conditions, equipment, etc. We do not apologize for this, but rather, feel strongly that it is necessary since most soaring references available in English definitely have a European, and, more specifically, a U.K. slant.

It was decided that we would write this book with detail on currently available equipment. We realize that this could make the book obsolete much quicker than if we had taken another tack, but we felt it was much better this way because readers want to know specifics about presently available equipment and we would rather keep this approach even though it means upgrading this text rather more often than would otherwise be necessary.

We would like to thank our many soaring friends who, knowingly and unknowingly, made the writing of this book possible. We have learned a lot from our teachers both in the air and on the ground, and we realize that this education is a continuing and never ending, but delightful process which makes our sport the tremendous challenge that it is. Specifically, we would like to thank soaring professors George Moffat, A. J. Smith, Dick Johnson, Ben Greene, and Dick Schreder, whose classrooms, both in the sky as well as on the ground, have been of great benefit in collecting material for this book.

Ed Byars
Bill Holbrook
1974

THE SPORT—HOW TO APPRECIATE IT

1.1   INTRODUCTION

To those who have been in the sport awhile, the word "soaring" is a vague and imprecise term. It encompasses almost the whole realm of motorless flight from just a cut above gliding off hills in a primary to include training, cross country, FAI badge flying and including the most sophisticated competition and record flying. Any book that attempted to cover completely all aspects of the sport would be too voluminous and would be a treatise indeed.

As the title "Soaring Cross Country" implies, this text covers only one phase of the sport. It might be considered an intermediate phase since it is presumed that the reader of this book has gone through most of the initial training stages but has not yet mastered the art-science of cross country soaring. We have attempted to refrain from presenting all of the tedious details which can be a part of this aspect of the sport. We try to strike a compromise balance which will present a maximum of useful, practical information in a non-technical, readable manner. We hope we have succeeded.

This introductory chapter includes a few comments about our basic philosophy and approach to this part of the sport.

1.2   LEVELS OF ATTAINMENT

Any sport worth its salt must have levels of attainment for its participants and each level must offer a new challenge. Soaring qualifies double in this respect. First the challenge of earning each qualification, licenses and badges; and second, the never-ending challenge of remaining aloft. The latter challenge never ceases to tax the best efforts of all sailplane pilots regardless of experience. Since soaring deals so intimately with nature and its unlimited variable conditions, there exists an infinite variety of situations to challenge the enthusiast.

The newcomers to the sport who now are at a level to be challenged by the subject of this book generally feel that the levels of attainment are tied closely to achievement of FAI badges. The more experienced in the sport know that the real achievement of a pilot is related to the task he sets for himself and how well he accomplishes that task. For example, a successful 50 kilometer Silver "C" cross country flight may be more challenging and represent a higher level of attainment on some days than a Diamond distance flight on other days.

The broad concept of the soaring sport stretches the mind of a pilot so his attainment will be tied to his level of knowledge of many diverse subjects. To approach the top he must work his way up in such disciplines as meteorology, low-speed aerodynamics, instrumentation, navigation, structures, strength of materials and a honing of a competitive spirit.

It is invariably true that top soaring pilots can speak intelligently about any of these areas of knowledge but none is foolish enough to consider himself a master of any of them. The joy and fun of the sport is in learning to increase our levels of competency.

1.3 DEGREE OF SAFETY

Being a part of aviation, soaring must suffer along with an uninformed lay public who have an inherent fear of aircraft and a belief that airplanes are basically unsafe. This is natural since aviation is only one generation old. There are many people who grew up with aviation and remember, all too well, the hectic and turbulent history that brought it to the advanced stage it is today. They have been adversely influenced by the news media which dwells on the unsafe and the gruesome, but newsworthy aspects of aviation.

Since you have already been flying gliders, you know that they are basically safe, with slow landing speeds, improved means for rate-of-descent control, are generally only flown in good weather, and obviously do not have a noisy fire hazard out front to worry about. No doubt, you are more concerned about safety now that you are considering flying a sailplane cross country, out of range of the obvious safe landing places at the airport. To our knowledge, no specific study has ever been made to determine what phases of soaring contribute most to accidents. It seems quite obvious to all who have been in the sport for awhile that most of the accidents in soaring in which people are hurt are not associated with cross country flight, but usually occur in training and flying in the vicinity of the airport. This probably comes from the fact that the people who fly cross country are more experienced and, in general, exercise better judgment. You will find that such things as structural failure or weather accidents are extremely rare, and that most soaring accidents represent poor judgment on the part of the pilot, usually while taking off or landing at an airport.

There is no question that landing a sailplane in a strange area away from the airport is more dangerous than on an airport. It is extremely rare that an experienced pilot gets hurt in an off-airport landing. All of the cross country and competition pilots that we have talked with about this are little concerned with physical harm to themselves when flying cross country. This is because the modern designed sailplane is extremely tough and most offer excellent pilot protection in case of accidents. It is not rare for a pilot to experience some damage to his sailplane in off-airport landings. Usually the harm done is very minor but once in a great while, it may be major. However, for anyone to even get a bump on the head when landing away is very unusual.

An honest analysis of bodily injury in soaring, as compared to all other sports, would show that soaring by no means ranks badly. In fact, we would bet that it ranks quite high in safety, considering the fact that it is a participation sport.

1.4 HIGH ENJOYMENT PER DOLLAR VALUE

You have been in soaring for awhile now and when people ask you, "Is soaring expensive?" you are probably hard pressed to answer in the negative. This matter of cost is always a relative one and it is not hard to name sports that are more expensive than soaring. Your non-soaring spouse, I am sure, can come back immediately with a dozen or so that are less expensive. It is hard for those of us who are really addicted to give an objective comment on the cost of soaring. We feel very strongly that soaring is very inexpensive when you consider the high value obtained on an "amount-of-enjoyment-per-dollar" basis.

There are three types of people in soaring; (1) those who are trying to promote the sport for the greatest number of the populace and who would like to see the costs low enough to induce the masses to join; (2) those who may or may not be able to afford soaring but are willing to accept the high cost and do not want to do anything to introduce the whole nation to the sport because they like the fraternal atmosphere soaring provides; and, of course, (3) the "in-betweeners" who promote controlled expansion. There are good arguments in favor of each group, but it should be obvious to everyone that the second group seems to be getting its way. You do not have to be in soaring very long to realize that there are relatively few young people in the sport. Those who are, are usually sons and daughters of avid soaring pilots. Incidentally, we don't consider the hang gliding movement a part of soaring. There is no question but that the expense keeps the bulk of the people away. There also is no question but that soaring, in spite of its steep growth curve in the past few years, is still a relatively exclusive sport.

You know by now how much the training portion of soaring costs and now you may be wondering about the costs of advanced soaring, such as cross country and competition. It is a hard thing on which to put a specific dollar value because it can vary tremendously with the degree of participation. It is not unusual for a top competition pilot to have $15,000 to $20,000 tied up in his equipment including his trailer, but exclusive of his car. He may trade sailplanes every two or three years and probably participates in one or two Regional contests, plus the Nationals every year. In addition to his capital outlay for equipment, his depreciation and expenses may cost from $2,000 to $5,000 a year. Compared with this top figure, we can point to club members who fly cross country out of their own home airport and share crewing duties with other club members while flying club equipment. Their expenses, including club dues, may be only a few hundred dollars a year; and their tasks may be just as challenging and their enjoyment of the sport may be just as high as that of the top competition pilot.

1.5   TEXT PHILOSOPHY

Getting back more specifically to what you will find in this text; we would like to make a few comments about our philosophy in presenting this material. It should be considered a non-scientific approach and more a presentation of ideas and philosophies rather than a great collection of details and theories.

After you have read this, you cannot go out with the book in one hand and the control stick in the other and soar across country by the numbers. We have tried to set forth some rather specific rules of thumb to use as guidelines; and, in a general way, discuss the influencing factors involved, rather than specific "flying technique" secrets.

Hopefully, after reading this book, your important soaring decisions will be based less on an intuitive hunch and more on the careful consideration of the relevant facts and intelligent assessments of the influencing parameters.

The whole sport of soaring is decisions. Important ones must be made on the ground as well as in the air. After reading this book, we hope you will be able to make them better. We try not to get involved in theory and details on such things as aerodynamics of sailplane flight, vortex theories of thermals, the theory of best speed to fly rings, etc. While these things are important to the competent cross country soaring pilot they are more adequately covered in other soaring texts and articles. Of course, references are given where appropriate.

We would expect and, indeed, recommend that the beginner read "The Joy of Soaring" and/or "The Art and Technique of Soaring" as part of his elementary soaring training. Then we hope you would study this book, after which we recommend the reading of more advanced and detailed texts such as "The American Soaring Handbook" and the excellent book which gives the English view, "The New Soaring Pilot" by the Welches and Irving: and, perhaps, "Gliding" by Piggott. The very serious advanced student will want a copy of "Meteorology for Soaring Pilots" by Wallington: and "Proceedings of the Symposium on Competitive Soaring" published by SOARING SYM-POSIA, and other similar references.

We do not deny that personal opinion is interwoven in this text; but we have tried to minimize it, especially as it relates to the commercial side of soaring. This is especially true in Chapter 9 on instruments and equipment, and in Chapter 10 Sailplane Selection. We hope you will realize that as many opinions as possible should be gathered before making decisions on which items of soaring equipment to buy.

PRE-FLIGHT PREPARATION
FOR SOARING CROSS COUNTRY

2.1   INTRODUCTION

The challenge of being far away from an airport in a powerless aircraft is exhilarating and the beauty of the countryside is incomparable when seen with the eyes of a great bird. An uneasy feeling of impending disaster bars the otherwise competent soaring pilot from turning his nose toward the open country and away from the comfortable nest of known thermal sources and the home field. A number of reasonable preparations on the ground and in the air around familiar areas will rid the pilot of these anxieties and give him a feeling of competence that will make the call of soaring great distances a beckoning he need not deny to himself.

Surely the greatest of these anxieties is the fear of damaging the sailplane in landing off an airport in some farm field and the liability assumed in landing on someone else's property. This anxiety will remain with a good pilot, but it is used to warn him to be cautious in his field selection—exacting in his pattern flying and approach speeds and meticulous in his planning and procedures. With these cares taken, off-field landings can be made regularly without damage to the sailplane or the farmer's property.

2.2   SPOT LANDING

Before attempting a cross country flight, the soaring pilot must be able to land the sailplane with precision on the spot he has selected. A good practice for this is to lay out on your home field a "practice farm field" such as that shown in Figure 2.1.

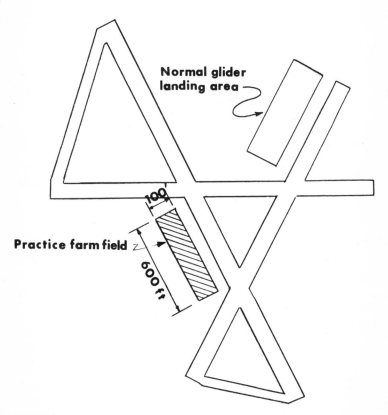

FIGURE 2.1

Figure 2.2 shows a seventeen-mile triangle laid out within

safe gliding range of the home airport. Over one-half of Silver "C" distance can be flown "cross country" without ever being more than 3½ miles from the "nest."

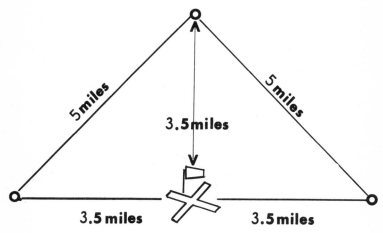

PRACTICE 17 MILE TRIANGLE
OVER ONE-HALF SILVER "C" DISTANCE.
AND NEVER MORE THAN 3½ MILES OUT!

FIGURE 2.2

Very good cross country experience can be gained by flying this small triangle. Work at flying such a triangle will teach proficiency in holding a heading, finding, entering and leaving thermals on course, and proceeding on course to a predetermined point, all basic factors in soaring cross country.

A little practice flying this triangle should enable the pilot to go around easily. Increasing the speed around the circuit improves efficiency in the basics. Limiting the maximum altitude of your climb sufficiently to force you to find more thermals is a good method of improving the cross country techniques and is used by championship pilots. After you have become proficient in spot landings in the practice area and can fly around the practice triangle with confidence, you can begin to consider heading out for your first venture at soaring cross country.

Find a friend with a power plane and have him fly you down the course you have selected at glider altitudes. This is the best kind of opportunity to become familiar with the landscape so important to your proposed flight.

Be sure to let your power pilot friend fly the airplane so you can devote full attention to simulating your flight in the sailplane. You prepare the map and do the navigating. Practice map reading—pick out the fields in which you think you can put a glider, have the pilot fly a glider pattern over some of these sites at an altitude low enough to determine if your selection was a safe one.

Practice using the landing away check list described in Chapter 6. Look for broad regions of good fields so you can alter course toward this area if you get a little low on your cross country venture; stretches where you would feel safe working a weak thermal at 1,000 feet.

Keep an eye out for the small towns, the factory sites, and the hills that are lift producing features.

Identify and study particularly your goal airport. If the airport is small and blends into the surrounding landscape, pick a prominent feature adjacent to it so you can fly toward this on your final glide even before you spot the airport.

The prediction of good soaring weather is an art that even the professional meteorologist will quickly admit requires a great deal of skill and luck. But the general weather patterns that produce good soaring in your area are worthy of very close study. Learn the features of these patterns and develop your ability to predict them.

An intimate knowledge and familiarity with your sailplane and equipment cannot be overemphasized. In addition to knowing your sailplane's flight characteristics, you should also become thoroughly familiar with all its accessories. The instruments, barograph, trailer, tow car, parachute and every piece of apparatus necessary for taking off—flying the course—landing—recording the results and then disassembling and retrieving safely, must be mastered.

Practice disassembling the glider on your home field before you have to do it in a strange plowed or muddy field, perhaps after dark at the end of a long day.

Are you confident about your barograph? Can you prepare it properly and be sure it is working while you are flying? Practice removing the trace and going through the procedure described in Chapter 6 required in completing it for transmittal to the S.S.A.

Swing your compass—know your variometer. Many fine flights have been made by good pilots with variometers that were slow and inaccurate, but these pilots understood the characteristics of their particular instruments.

Your practice in these details will build your confidence and allow you to concentrate on flying when that big day arrives for the distance flight.

2.3 MAP SELECTION AND PREPARATION

Sectional charts (1:500,000 scale) are designed for navigation by pilotage in slow speed aircraft and are the standard charts used in soaring cross country. A catalog of all U.S. civil charts as well as the monthly flyer "Dates of Latest Editions—Aeronautical Charts" may be obtained free from:

DISTRIBUTION DIVISION C-44
NATIONAL OCEAN SURVEY
RIVERDALE, MD. 20840

Don't use old charts. Towns don't move, but new high-ways spring up every year and old airports become shop-ping centers and industrial parks. The place you have chosen for a goal airport may not be an airport any more. If you are going to fly regularly, subscribe to the sectionals of the areas in which you are interested. The AOPA (Air-craft Owners & Pilots Association) has this service as do a number of other aviation organizations and dealers.

Practice plotting the latitude and longitude of points on a sectional chart. The S.S.A. badge applications, the State Soaring record forms and all contest distance points are based on the latitude and longitude of the take off, release, and landing points. Many experienced competition pilots are still not totally competent at this simple task.

When ordering charts, order an extra set for your crew to have with them when you call back with your position. Both you and your crew will then have the same map. Then teach them to read a sectional; the aeronautical sym-bols are very confusing to one accustomed to reading a road map. This saves a lot of added confusion, of which there always seems to be a plentiful supply at the beginning of a retrieve.

Navigating a sailplane cross country is complicated by several things not readily apparent. One of these is the lack of room in the cockpit to open the chart or to refold it or, for that matter, to store it. Try sitting in your sailplane on the ground with the canopy closed, all strapped in for flight, then unfold a sectional chart and refold it to see the portion showing your course line; all with one hand be-cause you must fly the ship with the other. This will quickly demonstrate the need for planning the folding and storing of your charts.

The variation in height of sailplane in flight from the top

of one thermal to the altitude where you intersect the next is also very different from normal airplane navigation. Plot your position carefully during your straight flights on course, note the exact compass heading of your desired course while at cruise so you can roll out on this heading again as you top out of the thermal. Be sure to write down the compass course of your flight for reference.

Draw and label circles on your chart of 5, 10, 15, 20, 30, 40, 50-mile radii from your landing point. Use a semi-thin felt point pen with a bright contrasting color (red or orange). These circles are very necessary in computing your final glide. Draw your anticipated flight path with a straight edge and mark one mile intervals for, at least, the final 20 miles along this line. You should, at any time during the flight, be able to glance at the map and position yourself on it and, by noting the previously drawn circles and mileage marks, tell exactly how many miles you are from your goal.

2.4   WEATHER

In preparation for your first cross country and as a good practice for all future flights, watch the best television weather forecaster in your TV area, particularly on the few days before your anticipated flight, for general background information. Then call your nearest aviation weather service, either the Weather Bureau or the F.A.A. Flight Service Station, on the day before you propose to go, for a forecast. You will then be thoroughly familiar with the general picture before you make the all-important call on the morning of the day of the flight.

2.5   EXTRA EQUIPMENT

In addition to your sailplane, barograph, trailer, and parachute, a number of small items are required of all entries in a national contest that make good sense and should be part of every cross country sailplane's equipment. They are:

1.   A first aid kit
2.   A tie down kit
3.   A quart of drinking water in addition to that carried for use in flight
4.   Some high-energy food—dried fruit, hard candy, Gatorade, etc.
5.   The tools essential to disassembling the sailplane
6.   Small flashlight

The first aid kit should contain a large triangle bandage, some spirits of ammonia inhalers and first aid cream. One more handy item that will save time is an extra set of fresh batteries for any electrical equipment you may have aboard. The batteries in the sailplane should be checked the night before the flight and a fresh set in the car saves a lot of late running around and searching when one is found to be too low in voltage for safe use.

2.6   PERSONAL CHECK LIST

We all have our own personal style when it comes to clothes, but no one will accompany you on your sailplane flights so you may as well dress comfortably. Be sure to take along a jacket (a nylon windbreaker will do in the hot summertime) for it gets cool in the evening while waiting for the crew and trailer. Wear shoes in which you can comfortably walk a good distance because this chore is the normal ending of a great cross country flight. Carry along some sun protection—a light hat and some sun lotion if you are sensitive to the sun. These are often needed at the end of short, disappointing flights while sitting in the middle of a pasture warding off domestic animals and waiting for help. Sun glasses, while not essential, add a lot of comfort and safety when flying toward the sun.

Be sure you carry along some cash and a couple of blank checks. Include in the papers you take with you the sailplane insurance facts, such as the name, address and phone number of your insurance agency. These should be kept in the sailplane as they attest to your financial responsibility when you land among strangers who may not be soaring enthusiasts.

Every active soaring pilot has a telephone credit card. Be sure to carry it with you and that your crew has the number so they can call the base as necessary. A nationally -recognized credit card often comes in mighty handy. Personal business cards are good to write addresses on and serve as an introduction to the many people you will meet and ask for favors at the end of your flight.

2.7   LANDING FORMS

The S.S.A. application form for F.A.I. badges should be part of the regular papers carried in your sailplane, together with S.S.A. Item No. 39, State Soaring Record Rules and Application Form (see Appendix for an example). Should you complete a badge leg or think that you have broken a record, these forms are necessary and the time to get the required signatures is while you are awaiting your crew's arrival. It is sometimes impossible to get a signature of a person who will certify your landing several days after the event—especially if this must be done by mail.

2.8   TELEPHONE NUMBERS

Set up a common telephone for you and your crew to use as an information center. Make sure it will be attended at all times until you and your crew call back to confirm you are together. As a point of courtesy and a rule requirement in sanctioned contests, you must call back to this control point when you and your crew are together. On long flights this could be late at night and the crew may still be searching for you or you may be together in some arena of joy celebrating your triumph, but the faithful person at the distant home port may still be worried and waiting to give that last little bit of info that will be needed to get you together. So call home and tell him the ship's on the trailer and thanks for the patient help.

2.9   PHYSIOLOGICAL CARE

Soaring is much more physically demanding than flying a light plane. The pilot must sit for an extended period of time in one position. Solo flying is the rule with the demand for constant attention all during the flight and good clear decision-making ability required at the end of the period of long, confined tension.

Train for the flight by cutting back on coffee and stimulants 24 hours before the flight. Void your bladder just prior to takeoff. Have a substantial breakfast for it will be a long time until the next regular meal. If your endurance is low, take along a relief tube. Keep in shape. Don't attempt these flights if you are not feeling fit. Tell your doctor or flight surgeon about your intentions if you have any doubts and take his advice. Make sure your sailplane is comfortable. Lumps and tight corners become pretty sore after a couple of hours in a tight cockpit.

2.10   CHECKLISTS

As you prepare for your flight, develop a series of checklists as outlined in the later chapters. Crew checklists—automobile checklist—trailer checklist—a sailplane equipment checklist in addition to the normal preflight checklist. Coordinate with your crew chief and complete these preparatory checklists on the day before your flight and early in the morning of the big day. They save delays and increase your probability of a good flight.

SOARING WEATHER ANALYSIS

3.1 INTRODUCTION

The close tie between soaring and meteorology is as old as the science of flight and the many excellent books on the subject cover it thoroughly so it would be very presumptuous for us to attempt to add significantly to this basic knowledge. Our effort then must be to show you how to best gain access to this wisdom so you can use it in your soaring cross country flights.

We recommend the following books as required study for the pilot seriously determined to succeed in soaring cross country:

Soaring Meteorology for Forecasters
Forecaster's Handbook Number 3
by Charles W. Lindsay and Stanley J. Lacy
U.S. Department of Commerce
National Weather Service
Limited Edition

American Soaring Handbook, Section 5
by Dr. Harner Selvidge

Aviation Weather
by William Nash of the
U.S. Weather Bureau
The U.S. Government Printing Office

Meteorology for Glider Pilots
by C. E. Wallington
Published by John Murray, London, England

Weather Flying
by Captain Robert N. Buck
Macmillan and Company, 1970

These are only five of a great number of books that are concerned with soaring weather, but they are texts by meteorologists and pilots of considerable stature that are easily understood by the less technically minded pilots.

3.2   BASIC REVIEW OF METEOROLOGY

Soaring weather forecasting is really an infant science for it concerns slight variations in atmospheric turbulence. It is really micrometeorology. Therefore, a soaring pilot must study the weather with the constant intensity of a research student. You must glean all you can from all available sources, apply this information, and then carefully record the results in your mind. There is very little available knowledge and man is almost completely ignorant of the small changes that occur hourly in the earth's ocean of air. We have been forced to learn to forecast major changes in weather and therefore have not had time to study such small things as light breezes or the effect of two degrees of temperature change over a field that has been mowed. So, as a beginning, let us review some basic meteorology that will be of some assistance in our further study.

The earth's atmosphere is a very thin mantle consisting principally of air and water vapor concentrated within ten miles of the surface but extending much higher in a thin gas of little consequence to glider pilots. The relationship between the air and the water as constantly modified by the heat of the sun is the subject with which we shall concern ourselves.

Air becomes more dense and heavier when cold. The water vapor contained in the air remains gaseous until the air becomes too dense to contain it then it becomes liquid or solid depending on the temperature.

When the water changes form it absorbs or dissipates heat. Now, mix all these facts together and they produce weather. "But how does this affect the sailplane pilot?" you may well ask. Let us have a look at a nice summer day.

Since the day begins at dawn, consider the atmosphere at that time. The air near the earth cooled during the night and became very dense, so dense, in fact, that it cannot contain the water vapor in the colder valleys so the water vapor has been forced to leave the air and has formed minute drops of liquid suspended within the air—fog.

The cold lower air is colder than the air aloft. Since we all know that the higher we go, the colder the air should be, this unusual phenomenon of cold lower air is a turned over or inverted condition, hence, it is called an inversion.

Since this inversion of cold air is relatively shallow, but heavy, it lays over the earth like a blanket which the upper winds cannot stir. Above this blanket, the whole atmospheric pressure patterns of the world move the air about as determined by the total heart balance of the earth-sun relationship.

The temperature falls at a rate of about 2° Centigrade (3.6° F.) per thousand feet of altitude and clouds form when the temperature of this air mass raises the density of the air to the saturation point and the water condenses, but our nice summer day is clear and beautiful without enough water vapor aloft to cause clouds.

As the sun rises and begins to heat the earth, we note the gradual changes in the air. The valleys become warmer and, therefore, the air in them less dense so the water can return to a gaseous form. The cold dense layer of the inversion begins to heat up from the warm earth and expand; the top now rises slowly so all of the water vapor and pollutants spread out and we can see between them. So the visibility begins to pick up.

Now comes the time of prime interest to the soaring pilot. As this cold air is warmed, it will reach a point when it is warmer than the air aloft. Not just a little warmer, but so warm it rises up into the colder air. When this occurs, it happens in bubbles or large columns from areas of the earth that were first heated and became even warmer than the surrounding ground. These bubbles of rising air cool as they rise because the pressure drops with altitude. Lower pressure—lower temperature is the rule.

The rate of cooling caused by the pressure drop of this parcel of air is called the dry *adiabatic* (aid-dea-batic) lapse rate. The normal rate the atmosphere cools with altitude is called the standard lapse rate. Note and mark well this point. The standard lapse rate is 2° Centigrade (3.6° F.) per thousand feet and the dry adiabatic lapse rate is over 3° Centigrade (5.4° F.) per thousand. So on a standard day the air is stable because as soon as it starts to rise, it cools to where it is colder than its surroundings and sinks back to where its temperature matches the rest of the air.

However, the day we are concerned with is to be a glorious soaring day for the temperature of the air aloft, up to an altitude of 8000 feet, is colder than standard by 3° Centigrade at each thousand foot level as determined by the upper air sounding. So as the first bubble of warmer air rises because it is a couple of degrees warmer than its surrounding air, it keeps rising as it continues to be a little warmer than the rest of the air despite the cooling caused by its expansion. But since it is only a degree or two warmer, its rise is slow and temperature difference is small. Even the slight mixing with the upper atmosphere cools it and destroys its lift.

When it left the earth, the remaining cold air moved into the void causing a light breeze to tell the soaring pilot that the first thermal activity has begun.

As the heat of the sun intensifies, the warming trend becomes more pronounced and the general cold air of the surface is warmed to a temperature well above that of the air aloft. Great streams of warm air rise from the hotter places on the surface and are replaced constantly or in pulses by the cold air from aloft now settling to replace it. This great mixing causes gusty surface winds especially in the vicinity of the heat sources and also allows the winds aloft to descend to and affect the surface that was formerly protected by the blanket of cold night air. The instant that this general lift begins is when the soaring day begins.

As the heat of the ground rises, the air on its surface also increases and the temperature difference between this surface air and the air aloft becomes greater. Therefore, the force of the rising air is stronger so the mixing as it rises is reduced and it goes to a greater height, finally reaching the area of stable air at perhaps the 8000 foot level. Now comes another interesting point; if this area of stable air begins at a height where the surface air cools to a temperature that causes the water vapor to condense—clouds—cumulus clouds of fair weather will form. These lovely clouds mark the top of the soarable air—if the air above this level is very stable. They also mark the top of the columns of rising air.

If a good heat source on the ground produces continual rising air and the general wind drifts these large long bubbles downwind, the result will be a series of cumulus clouds or a cloud street under which long straight flights can be made in rising air.

As the end of a long column of rising air finally reaches the top, the action stops—the cloud evaporates as it has no warm wet air to supply it. So there is no lift under a dying cumulus and you must now look for the sharp wisps that mark the beginning of a fresh cloud at the top of a new column of rising air.

Just suppose that on our lovely day the upper winds above 8000 feet have brought in some cold air so the rising surface thermal can continue above the level where the water vapor condensed. Should this happen, the most powerful force of all raises its head. The water vapor turns to liquid; liquid retains heat better than gas so the energy used to condense the vapor is retained in the liquid and the bubble cools at a lower rate. This new rate is called the wet adiabatic lapse rate.

Since the wet air remains warmer, it rises faster. As it rises faster, more water vapor condenses causing larger drops to form; drops are now raindrops and for a short while they remain suspended in the rapidly rising air but soon become so heavy they fall clear to the ground where they cool the surface so no more air rises, effectively shutting off soaring near this shower.

If the air aloft is more unstable, this action could cause a thunderstorm as the energy released when the water becomes frozen above the freezing line is tremendous. Since this is only a simple example to help you understand some of the better texts on cumulus and cumulonimbus development, we will alow you to delve deeper in these better texts for a complete understanding of this fascinating phenomenon.

Our soaring day nears the end of the cycle as the sun begins to set. The reduced heating allows the earth to cool and only the hotter sources produce thermals. Great stretches of the surface moderate in temperatures so thermals are far apart; but when they do occur, the warm rising air will still carry to 8000 feet—more slowly perhaps —but it can be fed by the residue of the warmer pockets carried to the source by the cooling air that is replacing it on the ground. This makes that last great evening thermal. The earth now cools evenly and the blanket of night air again begins to form.

3.3   PREDICTING SOARING WEATHER

The day described in the previous section is rather easily predictable as a good soaring day with the use of a few weather bureau aids such as lapse charts and winds aloft forecasts.

The lapse charts can be obtained from your nearest weather bureau. The American Soaring Handbook gives an excellent review for the non-technical pilot of their use. Basically, they tell you the stability of the air vertically through the atmosphere by plotting the temperature received from upper air soundings on a graph. With this plot, you can tell how warm the day must become for thermals to form and how high these thermals will rise.

The stability index is plotted by the weather bureau for various stations throughout the country, and can be used to give a general idea of the soaring potential of an air mass that may be moving into your area.

The winds aloft are given at 3000-foot levels beginning at 3000 feet above mean sea level. So for our general purpose, we are interested in the winds at the surface and up to 12,000 feet above the surface for thermal and ridge soaring and all the way up to the legal limit for wave flights. The wind data is forecast from actual soundings taken at various major weather bureau centers scattered about 200 miles apart throughout the country. The forecasts are fairly accurate above 10,000 feet but below that level they are not very dependable.

Some points to watch for in the use of the winds aloft to forecast soaring conditions are changes in velocity and changes in direction. Either of these can cause a phenomenon known as a wind shear. A wind shear will sometimes break up the rising air to the point where it is difficult to climb above the shear line. It will always make the thermal rougher and tougher to climb through at the shear band. Many times this is a consideration in picking the "height band" mentioned in Section 3, Chapter 5 (In-Flight Decisions). Once you are above the shear, the thermals will often smooth out and be even easier to work so, again, the advice to get high and stay high becomes valid. Wind shears often occur in mountainous regions at a level near the top of the highest ridges.

Good thermal soaring occurs when the winds aloft are below 25 knots and constant in direction and velocity. Higher winds make thermals difficult to work below 2000 feet above ground and are a serious navigation problem in any flight except directly downwind.

3.4   OBTAINING WEATHER INFORMATION

The obvious answer to this problem is to call the

weather bureau, but many misunderstandings exist about this simple solution.

First: An F.A.A. Flight Service Station (F.S.S.) is not a branch of the weather bureau. These fine, helpful people are airway traffic specialists with enough training in weather to take an official observation. They are not trained to forecast weather.

The weather given by F.A.A. flight service is read from a teletype machine or a computer printout. The forecasts and winds aloft given are prepared and transmitted from central National Weather Service forecast centers such as Washington, Miami, Kansas City, etc. Most large metropolitan airports have branches of the weather bureau to make local forecasts and take observations for aviation, agricultural, marine and other interests. These local weather bureaus are the best source of good data, especially if the meteorologists are interested in soaring weather as are a surprising number of them.

Visit them personally and ask them any general weather questions you might have. Then your calls will result in a great wealth of valuable information.

When calling any of these services, F.A.A. or the Weather Service, for weather, prepare for the call by having a large pad and a sharp pencil ready. Identify yourself as a soaring (glider) pilot, planning a flight from Able to Baker giving your anticipated takeoff and landing times. The attendant will then normally give you the terminal and area forecasts for stations along your route. Write these down even if you must ask him to repeat them. After he has finished his regular aviation briefing, ask and write down the following information:

1. The winds and temperatures aloft for the nearest

station that takes actual soundings located 50 miles or more upwind of your course. This will give you some idea of the air mass moving over the area of your flight.

2. The full present weather sequences and terminal forecasts of any stations located upwind of your flight including temperature, dew point, surface winds, and barometric pressure trend.

As you complete your call, give him your name and ship registration number for his records. Try to glean all the information you need and write it down. Leave the questions of theory of weather and philosophy of forecasting until you make your personal visit. These people have heard all the weather jokes and are very busy—so busy that it sometimes requires quite a long wait to get them to the telephone. So just get the data, but all the data, and hold the comments until you see them personally.

Many meteorologists keep records of soaring weather in their files so drop a postcard to them if their briefing preceded one of your more successful flights. They will appreciate it and it may help them improve their ability to communicate with the soaring fraternity.

3.5   WAVE WEATHER

Soaring in the rising currents of air mechanically lifted as the wind passed up the face of a steep hill was the first form of powerless flight. Thermal soaring did not begin until the Germans converted a variometer from its original use as a free balloon instrument to sailplanes in the late 1920s. During the middle '40s, the phenomenon of the Mountain Lee Wave was first explored for soaring potential and now provides rides to tremendous heights in beautiful clear cold air at some of the lovely mountain resort areas of the world.

Lee waves are generated as any fluid flows smoothly over a disruption on a surface. The simplest examples are the ripples downstream of a stone on a creek bed, or perhaps even a better example are those waves downstream of a drop of the floor of the stream.

Just as the water makes waves downstream of these obstructions, great streams of air make waves in the atmosphere as they pass over the mountain ranges of the earth. Since water is a liquid, its density is constant and as it always flows downhill, its direction is more nearly constant. However, air is a free gas of varying density, expanding and contracting, and moving in constantly changing directions; but when the air is stable and the flow consistent, laminar waves are formed. So the rule of forecasting waves is to watch for constant density of the air and constant direction and velocity over the mountain range.

This information can be gleaned from the weather data obtained as described in the previous section. Look for winds aloft of fairly consistent velocity, perhaps increasing with altitude at a rate of 5 knots or so per 3000 foot level, a very stable temperature gradient (that is one very close to the standard lapse rate of 6°C. temperature drop per 3000 foot level) and constant direction, and changing less than twenty degrees from 3000 feet to the top of the usable atmosphere.

Should the air at the surface be sufficiently unstable to produce thermals, the smooth flow will be disturbed and should the thermals rise above the height of the mountain range they can disrupt the flow completely. For this reason good wave flights are usually planned with a dawn takeoff as the cold stable air in the valleys acts as a smooth surface and allows the air to flow without disruption. The smoother the surface of the wave generating area, the more powerful the wave.

It must be mentioned that good wave flights have started with climb in thermals to an altitude where the wave becomes effective. These instances are not common, however.

Tips on wave flying techniques—a few wise proverbs on flight in a wave are:

1. Never turn downwind unless you want to come down. The lift band in a wave is usually rather narrow especially considering the velocity of the wind. So when you want to position yourself a little more downwind, merely slow to just above stall speed and drift backwards or turn up to 45° off the best heading and drift back.

2. Fly fast into the wind and try to penetrate upwind if the lift begins to decrease. Most pilots have a tendency to drift backward out of the wave when they are not familiar with this type of soaring.

3. Take an orientation ride in a two-place ship with a local experienced wave pilot. This saves several high and expensive tow fees while learning where the geographic area of the wave is located.

4. Have a good oxygen system and know how to use it. Waves can carry you to heights where there exists a very real danger of passing out from lack of oxygen.

5. Wrap up in plenty of warm clothes because wave flying is a very cold way to spend the day.

6. Beware of the closing window! On days when the wave window is the only hole in the clouds, be extremely careful for an extra amount of moisture carried into the system can cause it to cloud over in

a matter of minutes, trapping you on top. If in doubt, don't go up.

3.6   RIDGE SOARING

The lift caused by air being forced upward over an obstruction on the earth's surface is referred to as ridge lift. This is a thrilling way to fly a sailplane, but probably the most hazardous to the pilot inexperienced at mountain flying.

The reason for the danger is not apparent in the theoretical line drawings of ridge lift because these fail to show how close to the ridge you sometimes must fly to obtain lift. It is not unusual to find this lift only within 200 feet of the surface of the ridge and rarely will it lift you more than one-third of the height of the ridge above the top. So, on a 1000-foot cliff, the farthest you will normally be from the ground will be 300 feet when you are at the very top of the lift. The Creator did not make any classic ridges of great, uninterrupted length so soaring down a long ridge often means crossing small areas of discontinuity—a big word for sink areas. Since you are only a few hundred feet above the valley, these can cause great mental strain as a landing becomes a probability in a hurry.

The exploration of the ridge soaring potential of the central Allegheny Mountains was first recognized by Richard du Pont in 1933 but it was 35 years before Karl Streideick startled the world with his record out and return flight in a medium performance Schleicher Ka 8. The out and return distance records along this route must be recognized as the tops in ridge soaring and any writing about the subject should include an analysis of the technique pilots use to accomplish them.

Detailed planning is more valuable for ridge soaring

record distance flights than on any other record attempts. The course to be flown must be studied and plotted in detail for the route to be followed cannot vary as it follows the ridge line just as a ship follows a narrow channel. There may be alternate routes over short portions of the course but these must be carefully plotted and followed as planned or the pilot will find himself out on the end of a ridge that descends into a wooded canyon with no ridge ahead to jump to just as a ship might choose a dead-end channel. All of the world record flights along these ridges were first flown by the record-breaking pilots in power planes to review and confirm the terrain indicated on the charts.

The weather patterns that provided the constant wind flow over the total planned route must be studied so they can be forecast accurately at least 36 hours in advance of the flight period. Karl Streideick's analysis of the forecasting method he used is detailed in the "Proceedings of the 1972 Symposium on Competitive Soaring" and is well worth serious study by anyone interested in ridge and wave soaring in the eastern U.S.

One last limiting factor (other than biological) for record ridge flights is the daylight hours required versus those available. The sunset and sunrise tables give this information and also show why December and January are not the right months for the record attempts even though the number of days with the proper weather pattern are greatest during these winter months.

The surface winds on these record days sometime gust to 45 knots and the gust loads on the pilot and sailplane while well within the physical limits are a factor of serious concern. Flights in these wind conditions are very dangerous for the pilot not experienced in flying over mountainous terrain.

However, one use that even the inexperienced pilot can make of ridge lift is the art of picking up thermals on the upwind side of a ridge. The mechanical lifting of the general winds often moves the bubbles of warm valley air to a ridge and triggers an unstable condition producing a thermal. When low over the top of a ridge, stay just upwind in the lift and try to pick up these thermals.

Some ridge soaring rules are:

1. Never turn toward the ridge! Your airspeed plus the wind will carry you into the ground or over the hill in an instant.
2. Don't fly on the downwind side of a ridge. This is where the turbulence and down is located.
3. Don't ridge soar on days of reported surface winds above 15 knots and unstable air. This condition can cause turbulence of awesome proportions.
4. Talk to the local pilots about the peculiarity of "their" ridge.
5. Keep your airspeed at least 10 knots above "normal."

3.7   IN-FLIGHT WEATHER FORECASTING

Sailplane flights of long duration covering miles of distance frequently fly into changing weather patterns as the day progresses. The secret of successful long flights is recognizing these changes and adjusting your flight planning accordingly. The method of adjusting is covered in Chapter 5 on In-Flight Decisions. Here we would like to review some of the weather signs to watch for.

Clouds are the signposts in the sky; billboards might better describe them for they advertise the weather. We have discussed the puffy cumulus of fair weather—you will be fortunate if you find lift under one out of three of these even on a good day.

A rule to remember is that thermals are roughly five times as far apart as their height. So on the day of our example, the thermals will be about 30,000 feet or five miles apart. In West Texas where thermals reach 10,000 to 12,000 feet above the ground, it is not unusual to fly for 15 or more miles between them.

Cloud streets and long areas of thermal lift are not uncommon so try to recognize them and overcome a fascination with circling. Experienced pilots often fly segments of one-half hour or more without circling, often with a net gain in altitude.

Wet ground is bad news. It represents an irrigated area or the mark of a recent rain, recent rain being within the past 24 hours. Avoid these areas in your preflight planning and remember this when watching the television weather the night before your flight.

High, thin cirrus clouds complicate soaring weather. When they thicken, they shut off the heat and this usually draws the curtain on soaring weather. This thickening is often the sign of an approaching front so when you see a high cirrus cloud cover on the horizon, watch out.

Dust devils mark the base of a column of rapidly rising air. They are aptly named as many a pilot has flown to the ground chasing these elusive devils over the desert. They move rapidly over the ground in rather erratic patterns and dissolve as quickly as they form. Use them if they are close, but don't waste time trying to reach one from a distance of several miles.

Big blue holes with no clouds can mean one of two things; a more stable air mass—therefore, poorer weather for soaring, or; air of slightly less water vapor content so the thermal tops are not condensing into clouds. The only way to find out for sure which situation has caused the blue area is to venture into it at reduced speed and maximum L/D.

The pulsing of good thermal weather during certain days is not unusual. Sometimes 30 minutes to an hour of good thermals slowly turns into a period of equal time of quiet reduced activity. It seems as if the earth had expended its heat energy and is resting to build up for another long burst. Watch for this condition and try to be high at the end of the pulses.

In summary, any phenomenon that interferes with the heating of the earth is bad for soaring. Lift is where you find it. Don't try to make it fit your mental pattern, but fly to fit its pattern. Become a student of the weather and particularly of cloud forms. Remember, weather changes constantly, so be prepared for the change.

3.8   SEA BREEZE "FRONTS" AND SHEAR LINES

During the hot part of a day when the general winds aloft are light, the cool air over the ocean or a large body of water such as one of the Great Lakes will move inland across the shore to replace the warm air that is rising over the land. So, in effect, this becomes a low altitude cold front that progresses from the shore inland as the day becomes warmer. It is marked by a line of cumulus clouds formed parallel to the shore and furnishes a good source of lift in the area under the cu where the warm air is rising.

In the desert regions a similar phenomenon is not uncommon as cool air from some source such as broad irrigated areas moves in a mass across the hot desert to replace the general rising warm air. Since the air is very

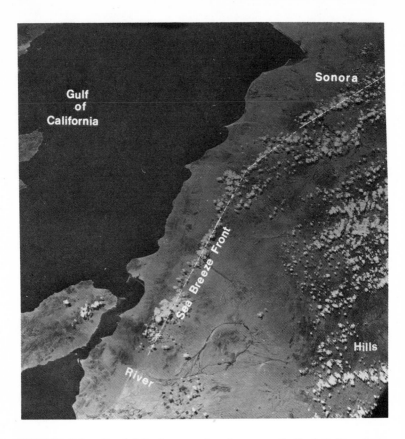

FIGURE 3.1 Gemini-5 photograph taken over Gulf of California at 2015Z, August 21, 1965, with Sonora, coast of Mexico on the right. The Sea Breeze front is clearly defined in this spectacular picture. The cold air from the Gulf of California has moved about five miles inland replacing the hot air rising from the desert. The rising hot air is popping off the top of the hills as evidenced by the cumulus development on the lower right side of the picture. The lift concentration for the sailplane pilot is under the line of clouds along this "front" and could probably sustain a long straight flight without circling. Notice that the popcorn Cu inland is over the higher darker ground and the river valley in the foreground is clear, obviously low damp areas even in the desert are poor thermal generators.

dry, no cumulus are formed, but this line is marked by the dense cold air with its gray hazy look sharply defined against the clear air of the desert. This line forms an excellent source of lift.

Both sea breeze fronts and shear lines offer good examples of lift sources that afford the chance to fly long distances without circling, thereby covering a great distance in a shorter time. Remember, speed is the name of the game; distance traveled per hour is what counts.

When flying these weather systems, keep in mind that the cold dense air is very stable and it is virtually impossible to get high enough in the lift to penetrate through this cold air to an area where lift might exist in the cold air mass. Remember the rule. You can't fly through a front.

3.9 WEATHER HAZARDS

Many aircraft accident reports fail to mention the primary cause of the accident. This causal factor is the mistake the pilot made in taking off in the first place. He wouldn't have had the accident if good judgment had been exercised and he had stayed on the ground.

This goes for glider pilots who get caught in thunderstorms, vicious rotor clouds, and destructive surface gusts. Consider again the ideal soaring day described in the beginning of this chapter. Note that the morning was calm and the afternoon offered the possibility of trouble from the weather. Thunderstorms could have developed; stronger winds aloft could have excited gusty surface winds of destructive force. So it pays to be wary for these signs of trouble:

1. Early development of towering cumulus clouds fore-

cast trouble later in the day when they "overdevelop" and grow to the rain stage. Remember the
potential of the wet adiabatic lapse rate.

2. Strong winds aloft at the lower levels just above the
    inversion mean trouble when the lift starts and the
    inversion disappears. Then these winds will add their
    power to the breezes caused by the thermal activity.

Rotor clouds are a third hazard and the best advice here
is to listen to the experienced local pilots—both glider and
tow. A good rule to follow any time is don't go if the tow
pilot is doubtful of the safety of the flight.

Rotors are the mixed up rolling air (turbulent rather
than laminar) directly under the wave. Sometimes they are
marked by cloud but not always. This rotor mixes the
warmed surface air with the air aloft—it can touch the
ground and cause strong surface winds in exactly the
opposite direction of the wave flow. The shear between the
rotor and the smooth wave can cause towing incidents that
are more impressive than the flight in the wave. This is
another reason for an orientation ride at a strange wave site.

3.10   SUMMARY

Here are some of the important facts and tips given in
this chapter as a list to memorize:

1. Air becomes more dense and heavier when cold.
2. Cumulus clouds mark the tops of rising warm air
    columns (thermals). After you have forgotten the
    exact figures, just remember this fact and re-study
    cumulus cloud development to serve as a reminder.
3. Warm air goes up—cold air comes down.
4. F.A.A. Flight Service Stations are not branch
    weather bureaus.

5. Take an orientation ride at all strange wave soaring sites.

6. Never turn downwind in a wave unless you want to come down.

7. Never turn into a ridge.

8. Wet ground means poor thermal lift.

9. Weather changes constantly so be a student of these changes.

10. You can't go through a front.

11. Stay away from rapidly building and mature towering cumulus.

12. Don't take off if you think a dangerous situation may exist.

13. Only one out of three cumulus clouds produce workable lift.

14. Thermals are at least five times as far apart as they are high.

15. Don't chase distant dust devils.

16. Approach changing weather conditions cautiously.

17. Don't fly on the downwind side of a ridge.

TASK SELECTION

4.1 INTRODUCTION

The selection of a task for each sailplane flight is extremely important. In this chapter we will discuss why setting a task is important, as well as some of the types of tasks to be chosen, and how they should be chosen. Of course, the actual flying of the tasks will be discussed in other chapters. A well-trained sailplane pilot knows that a task is an important first part of considering any sailplane flight. It is very unusual for any competent sailplane pilot, particularly a competition pilot, to plan any sailplane flight without first a consideration of what specific task the flight will have.

4.2 NEED FOR TASK SETTING

In the immediate post elementary training period of each sailplane pilot, there is a great urge to fly the sailplane just to see if you can make it stay up without any other thought or task than this: Simply staying aloft. Since many sailplane pilots do not get any additional advanced training beyond this point, it is natural that they sometimes keep aimlessly flying around the airport at the tops of thermals until they finally become bored with the sport and drop out.

Although we cannot rule out an occasional introductory passenger hop, we also cannot emphasize too strongly the fact that aimless flying around the airport develops very bad soaring habits. Specifically, if you do not make yourself a challenging task for each flight, you will not:

1. Strive for optimum climb
2. Center thermals as well
3. Leave thermals at correct time
4. Leave thermals correctly
5. Enter thermals correctly
6. Fly at optimum speed
7. Learn to be time conscious

These seven skills are necessary to be an efficient cross country soaring pilot and will be dealt with in more detail in the following chapters in this book.

4.3   TYPES OF TASKS

The F.A.I. badges make an excellent progression of tasks and are the most common measure of performance and progress. The particular badge requirements will be detailed in another chapter. In commenting generally on the F.A.I. badge tasks, most experienced pilots agree that the altitude legs are rather meaningless and so is the five-hour duration; but we must agree that they are good practice for beginners. The F.A.I. goal and distance are somewhat better. The beginning sailplane pilot can get accustomed to flying tasks which are not as ambitious as any of the F.A.I. tasks and may progress considerably beyond these F.A.I. tasks in gaining experience.

The three important types of tasks in sailplane flying are triangles, goal and return, and distance. A general comment on each is in order. Triangles are popular in that they are easy on the crew. The sailplane pilot generally (hopefully) ends up back where he started from. In laying out triangular tasks, you should usually adhere to the 28 percent rule (which will be discussed in detail later) whether or not a State or other type record is being attempted. Goal and return tasks are also good for the crew's sake for the same reason and may be better than triangles in some instances, particularly when certain anticipated terrain or weather conditions must be fitted. Distance tasks are worse for the crew and the retrieve. They are, however, best for maximum distance if no air mass change is anticipated en route, or if the terrain downwind permits a distance task.

Any pilot who aspires to be a top competition pilot must concentrate on triangles and goal and return tasks.

4.4   TERRAIN SELECTION

This, and the next few sections of this chapter, will discuss some particular aspects of task selection. One of the first is the terrain in the area in which the task is chosen. Naturally, areas with more landing sites are best. In the eastern United States, goal and returns are popular parallel to the ridges (generally crosswind) where you can fly over ridges, which are good lift sources, and stay in range of the valley landing areas.

Close to the coast or other large bodies of water, triangles may be required, particularly if you are on a peninsula or if the water is close to the downwind side.

It is a good idea, generally speaking, to plan the task over high ground where lift is better with good landing valleys adjacent to your planned route. Obviously, one should avoid large areas of rough terrain if at all possible. A good suggestion is to survey the general areas around your soaring site with a power plane as much as possible. It always helps to be familiar with peculiarities in terrain in your area. In flying out of Cumberland, Maryland, for example, we have favorite valleys that we like to fly up and down, certain narrow valleys with poor fields that we generally avoid, and other areas of extremely rough terrain that we religiously avoid.

4.5   WIND CONSIDERATIONS

If you have a choice, it is generally a good idea to fly the downwind leg of a triangle or goal and return task first. This may not always be true for a very short task in the middle of a strong day, but ordinarily, if you start early, it is better to drift while climbing before conditions get strong. Downwind leg first means you spend less time climbing while drifting backwards because all or part of your last upwind leg is a final glide home. In contests, you usually do not have a choice except with distance tasks.

When flying into a turnpoint, go into an upwind turnpoint low and into a downwind turnpoint high. This will enable you to take advantage of the drift while climbing which may help you considerably to complete a task.

In selecting tasks, look for legs with ridge lift potential or wave possibilities. This would be a task parallel to a ridge, which is perpendicular to the wind.

4.6   NAVIGATION REQUIREMENTS

In selecting a task, study carefully to see if there is a choice whereby a task can be selected over terrain where navigation is easy, for example, where prominent landmarks exist and where terrain features are plentiful. This can vary greatly with the general topography and geography of the area in which you fly. Pilots who are accustomed to flying in the Midwest, where they either follow the section lines or maintain a constant angle with these lines, sometimes get uptight when they go east or west and must fly in the mountains.

If you are laying out some initial practice tasks, there is nothing wrong with taking advantage of a good interstate highway. These and other similar excellent landmarks are always welcome on a flight, especially when the visibility is limited.

Ease of navigation requirements for a task are not as important as good terrain or even as important as wind orientation selection.

If your experience level is such that you are not positive you can navigate with little trouble with a sectional map while soaring, then this topic of selection for navigational ease is more important until such time as more experience is gained.

In summary, it should be emphasized (and we hope you will agree) that soaring around the airport on the tops of thermals soon loses its challenge whereas the completion of even a small or short soaring task that taxes your soaring abilities is one of the most satisfying experiences to be had in soaring. Completing tasks is really what the sport is all about.

IN-FLIGHT DECISIONS

5.1 INTRODUCTION

The crux of soaring cross country is decisions. Many are crucial but none are more crucial than those made while in flight. Some very important decisions must be made prior to takeoff, such as those of task selection and pre-flight planning discussed in earlier chapters. This chapter will concentrate on decisions made after release and before landing. Those discussed here may overlap somewhat those discussed in the Landing Away chapter.

First, we must make one thing clear. *This is a racing sport.* Don't kid yourself that it's not. Any cross country soaring flight, with few exceptions, is a race against time. This is true of distance flights as well as speed tasks. Maximizing distance means maximizing speed in the fixed time available for the flight.

You should, therefore, keep well in mind that all in-flight soaring decisions, other than safety decisions, are based on covering the most ground in the shortest time; conserving the most number of seconds, etc. Any good soaring pilot becomes very time conscious early in the game. This is an absolute necessity for success in this game. We are, of course, discounting the rare pilot who is satisfied to soar around the airport on Sunday afternoons at the tops of thermàls. Since the subject of this book is soaring cross country, we assume that you pilots are no longer challenged by just staying up. You, presumably, wish to taste this cross country part of the sport and now realize wherein lies the real challenge and the real fun.

5.2   DECISIONS JUST OFF TOW

The first decision you must make in the air is to decide not to release early regardless of being towed through a big boomer. Of course, you should mentally mark these thermals but, in general, almost all experienced pilots agree that there is hardly ever any instance where it is not in your best interests to take the full 2000 feet tow. This is doubly vital in a contest because landing back at the airport usually means waiting at the end of the takeoff line. It can throw your timing off for the day and cost you valuable points.

The second major and important decision that you should make in the air immediately after release is to stay with any lift you have when you are below 2000 feet unless, of course, you are drifting out of airport range.

The third major decision is to decide not to leave the airport until you are sure you can stay up. We realize that you can never be absolutely sure but in this case we mean at least 95 percent sure. It is always a good idea to get the feel of the air and watch other ships carefully before getting brave in this respect.

5.3   HEIGHT BAND

The next series of decisions will be those extremely important ones made while en route soaring cross country. You must try to form, continually revise, and relate to your position at any instant, a mental picture of your overall flight as it relates to the accomplishment of the predetermined task. The height band is an important consideration in the progress of your flight. Let us start with a definition.

The height band is the altitude range within which you should fly. It extends from a safe low level up to cloud base or to a height at which the lift has weakened and to where it is not in the best interests of the flight to continue climbing. Later we will discuss in detail how to determine the lower and upper limits of this band. The limits of the height band are influenced not only by the strength of the lift which is, in turn, a function of the time of day, weather, etc., but also by the terrain, clouds, visibility, task length, and other factors which will be detailed later.

5.4   WHEN TO GO (TOP OF HEIGHT BAND)

The biggest mistake of beginning cross country soaring pilots is staying in a thermal too long, that is, after it is no longer efficient to do so. This is a natural mistake since the first thing that any glider pilot learns is to climb as high as he can, period. This is not wrong when a pilot is learning— in fact, it is very important for a soaring pilot to know how the top of a dry thermal feels and how to identify it.

A big and important step, however, is to learn to leave a thermal when it is still "good" but not good enough to maximize your speed.

Let's get specific now and give a general rule of thumb about the top of the height band, or, in other words, what is involved in making the decision to go or when to leave the thermal. In the middle of a good day, on a medium task, when the thermal tops or cloud bases are, say, at least

4000 to 6000 feet above the ground, you should leave a thermal when you are in the upper part and the lift drops to about 70 or 80 percent of the maximum value for more than a turn or two. You had better re-read the last sentence a time or two and let it sink in.

This is, admittedly, a general rule but at least it should be put down in writing so that you will have some guideline for a beginning. However, we must immediately say that many variables influence this 70 to 80 percent figure. It is based on the assumption that you can move at your best speed to fly to the next thermal and contact and maintain the maximum lift again. This percentage figure would be modified down (maybe drastically) if:

1. Cloud pattern ahead did not look as good.
2. Overcast ahead.
3. Thunderstorm or cu-nim shadow ahead.
4. Rougher or higher terrain ahead.
5. Wet terrain ahead.
6. Turnpoint ahead.
7. Time to start final glide.

On many days with cumulus clouds, the thermal strength increases up to and into the base of the clouds. In this case the top of the height band then becomes the cloud base. Of course, we feel compelled here to mention that you should observe the legal vertical proximity to clouds which the F.A.R. will allow.

In deciding how much the seven above mentioned items will influence the top of the height band is a matter of judgment depending on each individual case. This judgment is developed with experience. In general, the less experience a pilot has, the more conservative he is. If things look different ahead, the pilot with less experience will tend to fly higher before he makes the decision to go. This is correct and natural. The judgment that is involved here is usually the separating factor between champions and almost champions. We will have more to say about these influencing factors later.

5.5   HEIGHT BAND VS. TIME OF DAY

The time of day influences many important parameters of a sailplane flight, not the least of which is the height band. So that we might better improve our mental picture of how these important parameters vary with time of day, a few sketches might be in order.

First, study Fig. 5.1 which shows how the lift may vary with time of day on a good day. The specific numbers for lift are not particularly important. What is more important is that you develop a feel for the fact that lift will increase rather abruptly once it starts in the morning and will end

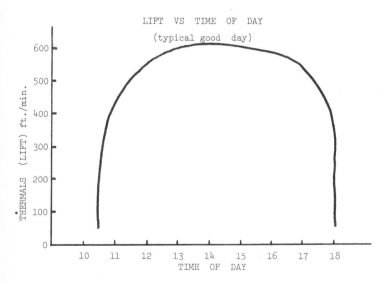

FIGURE 5.1

rather abruptly once it starts to quit at the end of the day. Notice in Fig. 5.2 that not only does the thermal strength vary with time of day but so does the thermal height, that is, the tops of the thermals vary with the time of day. We see in Fig. 5.2 that the tops may be only 2000 to 3000 feet when the thermals first start in the morning and slowly rise until the middle of the day at which time they generally stay rather constant until the end of the day when they quit. Many times when you can find that last late evening thermal, the top is often as high as any have been all day.

Remembering that these figures represent a typical good day not influenced by any sudden air mass changes or

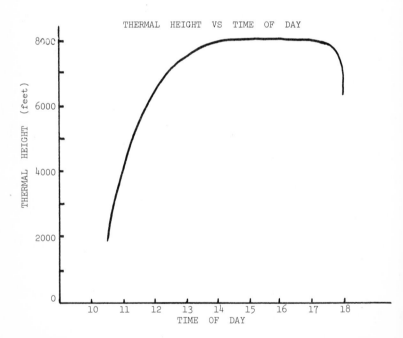

FIGURE 5.2

other abrupt factors, let us look at Fig. 5.3, which is a
typical plot of the height band vs. time of day. Notice
carefully that the solid line represents the tops of the
thermals vs. time of day and the upper dashed line
indicates the top of the height band which, of course, is
some percentage below the tops of the thermals as we
indicated earlier.

Again, let us remind you that these figures are rather
qualitative in nature and the specific numbers on the curves
may not be valid but the overall figure does show typical
trends. This figure assumes no clouds because the top of
the height band is limited by cloud base on many days.

A fact emphasized by Fig. 5.3 is that if you should have
reason to fly at the very beginning of the day such as you
might on a distance task, notice the height band is very

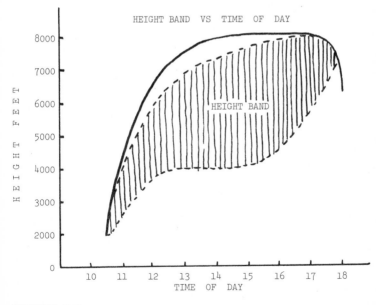

FIGURE 5.3

narrow at that time and the top is practically at the top of
the thermal. As the day gets better and the lift increases,
the thermal tops get higher. The height band, therefore,
broadens and the difference in height between the thermal
top and the height band top also broadens. Another
important consideration is that toward the end of the day
when conditions begin to "soften up," the top of the
height band again goes to the top of the thermal, the
bottom of the height band moves up rather rapidly and
you become more conservative. *There is no substitute for
being high at the end of the day!*

Remembering that Fig. 5.3 is time of day vs. height, let
us look at Fig. 5.4, which is time of day vs. climb rate. Do
not confuse the vertical axis (climb rate) with the height in
feet in Fig. 5.3 or the thermal strength shown in Fig. 5.2.

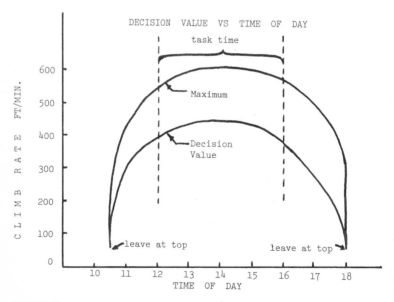

FIGURE 5.4

Climb rate is related to thermal strength in that we try to make our climb rate as high a percentage of the thermal strength as possible. This is a function of our ability to utilize the thermal most efficiently. It is very important to get a good mental picture and a good physical feeling for the true climb rate. Many pilots actually use a stopwatch to time their altitude gain over a period of one minute, to determine their net climb rate. It is difficult to watch the variometer and do an accurate mental averaging computation.

We tend to think that our net climb rate is the maximum that the variometer reads at any time during the last several circles. This gives an erroneously high estimate of the net rate of climb. Some sophisticated variometers have an integrating circuit which totalizes the variometer readings and gives a net climb rate readout directly. Let's assume that we do not have one of these goodies so we have to make some sort of intelligent estimate. Now back to Fig. 5.4 for some concentrated study. The upper curve is the maximum climb rate that we can achieve in a thermal at any specific time of day (the specific time of day is indicated by a vertical dashed line). The bottom curve represents the rate of climb at which we should decide to leave the thermal or the minimum acceptable rate of climb. In other words, how much must the lift drop off in a thermal before we make a decision to leave? This gets back to the big decision we referred to in the previous section. In the case of this figure, and for the purposes of our study here, we are assuming that things look good ahead and this decision is not influenced by any of the seven parameters mentioned in the "When to go" section (5.4).

Fig. 5.4 shows that at the beginning of the day when the

thermals are just starting, our net climb rate is very low and the two curves are together, so we should decide to be patient and leave the thermal at the top. In the middle of the day when the lift is strongest, we make our decision to leave the thermal when the lift drops to about ¾ of the maximum. At the end of the day we again should make the decision to stay in the thermal all the way to the top as the two curves are together and the net climb rate is again quite low.

A few other very important observations can be made from studying these figures. Study them carefully and see if you can understand why during the early part of a distance day, a turn or two at zero sink at the top of a thermal may be called for but such a thing later in the day would be wasteful and therefore intolerable.

Tasks such as speed triangles and out and return can be assumed to require a fixed length of time. Considering the meteorological and other conditions, an estimate should be made of how long the particular task should take and after adding a little margin, this length of time should then be fitted on the time of day scale of the above figures. As an example, the length of time between the two dashed vertical lines in Fig. 5.4 would be a typical assumed task time. It would be obviously prudent to utilize the strongest portion of the day for your task. On such a day, first climb to the top of a thermal to check the thermal height and the loss of lift at the top. This is commonly done in competition before going through the starting gate. It is not uncommon in contests or on speed record attempts to take off an hour or so before the anticipated start time. This hour is spent evaluating the thermal height and size as well as how the lift varies in the thermals.

From a study of the figures, notice that from middle to late afternoon we should be on guard for "softness" in thermals and a little less "character" to the clouds. When this condition is suspected, we ease the height band up (both the top and the bottom of the band) and as conditions continue to fade, we narrow the band upward all the way to the top. This would be true on a distance day then, hopefully, at the end of the day you would be at the top of the last afternoon thermal and ready to start a final glide at maximum L/D speed. An important and well proven axiom in soaring is: *"Stay high at the end of the day"* (if you can!).

5.6   WHEN TO STOP AND CLIMB (BOTTOM OF HEIGHT BAND)

We have discussed the major decision of when to leave a thermal and also should by now have some feeling for how the height band decisions would vary with the time of day. Let us now think about the equally important decision of when to stop and climb. This might better be called how to keep from flying into the ground. There is no more sickening feeling than to realize, too late, that you should have stopped and circled about a mile or two further back and 500 feet higher. This great decision has caused gray hair to appear on many a soaring head. We wish there were some magic answer we could give which would set a specific number that you could memorize and to which you could always adhere; but as you have no doubt guessed, such a pat answer does not exist. All we can do is discuss the influencing parameters and conditions and attempt to help you make better judgments.

Without beating around the bush any longer, we will go out on a limb with a general rule of thumb, as follows: In the best part of a good day, with numerous thermals looking good ahead (terrain, clouds, etc.), don't stop for any thermal (of course slow down while going through) if you have descended only a few hundred feet (or maybe 1000 feet) below the altitude you left the last thermal. An exception would be if the lift in the thermal core, as measured by your well-compensated (total energy) vario, tells you that it is significantly stronger (at least 150 percent) than the last core you worked. Now, go back and read the last two sentences several times and meditate carefully about it.

Suppose it is not a good day, or suppose it doesn't look too red hot ahead. Then, the influencing factors raise their ugly heads and we must become more cautious. The altitude to stop and thermal then depends on:

1.   Clouds ahead (good cu vs. dissipating cu vs. overcast, etc.).
2.   Terrain ahead (available landing places).
3.   Terrain ahead (likelihood of good thermal sources).
4.   Turnpoint or goal ahead.
5.   Time of day.

In summary, the decision as to when to stop and start climbing depends on your chances of getting back up or landing safely. Some pilots have rules such as working any lift below 2000 feet or maybe later in the day work anything below 3000 feet. Such a rule would be unthinkably conservative for top ranked competition pilots in some areas of the country under strong conditions on a good day. Of course, in other parts of the country on a lousy day, these figures may be somewhat rash.

5.7   WHEN TO HOLD

In the normal progression of a cross country soaring

flight, a rhythm is usually set up whereby one climbs and penetrates, climbs and penetrates, and this continual progression of events tends to get a groovy feeling about it which experienced soaring pilots refer to as the rhythm of a flight. When things are going well, this rhythm is unbroken but more often than we like to think about, something comes up to break this rhythm. Sometimes it is a poor decision at the bottom of the height band which gets us into a low scrape from which it takes time to recover (and, of course, from which we sometimes don't recover, and land away) and this breaks the rhythm. Sometimes for some reasons we choose to break the rhythm at the top of the height band and this is what we refer to as a hold. This is also when we move the height band up abruptly and it usually has to do with what things look like further along the course.

The only excuse for holding is the belief that conditions ahead will improve. Inexperienced pilots sometimes hold at the top of a thermal while making a decision. We are not referring here to this type of hold. The experienced sailplane pilot makes his decisions about the next cruise leg while he is climbing. The type of hold we are referring to is a waiting process in anticipation of conditions improving ahead.

To hold means to mark time. It means losing valuable seconds, which in turn means to either lose distance or speed for the day. That is why you should never hold unless you feel it will save you time in the long run, or that it will enable you to get more distance for the day.

Practically, the only reason for holding is to await a change in the weather. Weather conditions which might possibly warrant consideration for a hold would be an overcast, a blue hole, a thunderstorm, or, perhaps, a front. It is generally better to consider a detour instead of a hold if the detour will maximize your measured distance or minimize your time. Generally, the sooner a detour decision can be made, the better.

As previously stated, an experienced pilot will make this decision to detour while he is climbing. Pilots holding at the top of a thermal while in the thinking process can take a long time deciding. This is an intolerable waste of time if there is an opportunity of moving on and continuing the flight by means of a detour. A detour may be necessary for reasons other than weather, such as wet terrain ahead as in the case of irrigation areas or bad terrain features such as complete lack of landing areas.

If the weather ahead blocks the progress of the flight, then, a climb to absolute maximum possible height is in order so there may be no great haste in leaving the top of the thermal and starting a final glide. If bad soaring weather is moving toward you then a rapid climb as high as possible should be made and the penetration into the poor weather for maximum distance should be begun as soon as possible. By penetration into bad weather we don't mean into cloud or into gusty surface winds that would make landing dangerous.

Let us repeat here, again, that this is a racing sport and all of these in-flight decisions will be based on how it will influence maximizing distance and minimizing time.

5.8 CLIMBING TECHNIQUE VS. ALTITUDE

We assume that you have learned general climbing techniques in training and from practice. So it is in order now to make a few comments about how this climbing technique may vary with altitude.

In most instances the diameter of a thermal will increase with altitude. When you are low in the bottom portions of the thermal, it is usually necessary to fly at steeper angles of bank. Don't be afraid to rack it up to 45 or more degrees angle of bank when you're down below 2000 feet. This may be necessary to stay in the core. For safety, of course, it will be necessary to increase the air speed at these greater angles of bank, especially at low altitudes. When the cores are small, it is quite common to use 45 to 60 degrees of bank to maximize the climb rate. Lest we give the wrong idea, we must emphasize quite strongly that you should always use the *minimum* angle of bank possible to stay in the core. The less the angle of bank, the more efficient the sailplane and the lower the stalling speed.

The angle of bank may be quite shallow near the cloud base where the thermal diameter is larger.

You should practice low altitude thermaling near the airport but away from the pattern and not in any area of heavy traffic. It is certainly *not* recommended that you thermal with extremely steep angles of bank in gusty weather below 500 feet. As in all other phases of soaring good judgment must always be exercised.

Incidentally, here is a good place to reiterate the fact that you should not become left-handed or right-handed in soaring. All good soaring pilots are ambidextrous; that is to say, they can circle with equal ease either to the right or to the left. If you are more one sided this way, then you should make special efforts to practice the other way. Your in-flight decision as to which way to turn upon entering the thermal should be dictated entirely by the direction that will more quickly center you in the core and yield the best climb rate.

5.9 FINDING LIFT

Unfortunately, many sailplane pilots seem to think that the best way to find lift is by radio (asking others). Believe us when we say that this is "Sunday afternoon around the airport" stuff. It is very, very rare indeed that the pilot soaring cross country is able to get any help on the radio. It is against the rules in contests and soaring for records, and there are few other times when this type of help is available. It is best just to forget about this form of radio aid.

Cumulus clouds are still the best overall soaring indicators. When you are high, that is, within a thousand or two feet of the cloud bases, then you can use the clouds more directly for finding lift. It is important to learn to recognize growing cumulus clouds, as opposed to decaying cumulus.

All soaring pilots have at one time or another been frustrated by flying to a beautiful-looking cloud only to have it decay and become useless upon their arrival. It always behooves a cross country soaring pilot to study the clouds, particularly their growth patterns. Cumulus clouds start with a wisp, and it is generally much better to go toward a beginning wisp in search of lift rather than toward the full grown cu. If you notice a big blue area ahead, then study this area very carefully for evidence of beginning of wisps. Blue holes are not always bad in soaring. If they contain any inkling of a wisp, then they probably won't remain blue holes long. They are actually areas which should attract you in your search for lift. The final stage of a decaying cu is also a wisp so you must be careful to go for the starting wisp and not the ending wisp!

Which side of the cloud to go to? Upwind? Downwind?

Sunny side? The answers to these questions vary with many conditions, for example, the particular type of air mass, the season, the terrain, time of day, surface wind, etc. About the only thing that you can say for sure is that it won't always be the same each time. The best advice is to experiment. If you click once, then do the same thing or go to the same general area of the cloud again, and as long as you are successful, don't change your pattern. Most experienced pilots agree in general that you should try under the darkest area of the bottom of a cloud first.

Remember that thermals may slope considerably from the ground up to where they start to form the cloud. If you are very much below the cloud base, then it's quite reasonable to assume that the thermal may not be directly below the cloud, especially if the winds aloft are appreciable. Here, again, we must conjure up a mental picture of where the thermal is with respect to the cloud, and as is so often the case in soaring, we continually adjust this mental picture till we find success. Since the thermal tends to slope downwind, then you should search upwind of the cloud if you are much below it.

Not all clouds are good for finding lift in cross country soaring. The sun must get through to heat the ground. Cumulus can overdevelop and shut out the sun. In searching for lift, even up high, study the ground. If the cloud shadows begin to cover too high a percentage of the ground—WATCH OUT! High cirrus clouds can thicken seemingly without warning and shut out the sun. Keep an eye out for this condition in your search for lift.

Another common means for finding lift is the utilization of other sailplanes. Most championship pilots say emphatically that gaggles are bad. A gaggle is defined as a group of sailplanes in one thermal. For the less experienced cross country pilot, we would suggest that gaggles are not always bad but should be used with discretion. If you are in search of lift and see a high performance sailplane ahead making tight circles with a steep angle of bank, you can bet that he probably has a good core centered and there is no reason whatsoever that you should not share his good fortune, particularly if you know and respect the pilot. It is a well-known fact in competition circles that most pilots memorize and some actually make lists of the most competent pilots and their ship numbers so they will know which ships to follow. I think that we are making the point quite obvious when we say that if you, while soaring cross country, should come across a ship with a large number 2 or with XX on the tail, then it would be a good idea to watch it closely. Chances are he will show you some lift. In case you didn't recognize these championship numbers, they belong to America's two World Champion pilots A. J. Smith and George Moffat, respectively.

Other sailplanes can be especially helpful on a blue day with no clouds. A good trick utilized by many pilots is to follow along behind and several span widths to the side of a good ship and watch when he bobs up (an indication that he is slowing down in lift). When he does, then you move over and fly through the same good air that he has just been through. When he bobs down, indicating that he is going through bad air, then you move farther out and avoid this down area.

Pilots often discuss in detail the different aspects of team flying when looking for ways to improve their cross country soaring performance. The more experienced pilots generally agree that team flying is extremely tricky and will usually slow one of the participants down considerably.

This is not to say that it hasn't been utilized effectively at times, but it requires a great amount of experience and practice and, of course, identical equipment.

We have spent the last few paragraphs discussing how to find lift when you are up high. In these cases there is less anxiety in finding lift. Now let's discuss some aspects of finding lift when you are low. It is an understatement to say that soaring does have its anxious moments. There is no time more anxious than when you are down low and need to find lift badly to prevent a landing. As you sink from the middle altitudes to the lower altitudes, anxiety has a way of increasing exponentially. When you have trained yourself properly and have gained some experience, you can think more intelligently during this time of utmost stress.

The lower you drop away from cloud base, the less help clouds will be in finding lift. Cloud areas in general are still a good idea but, again, it should be remembered that thermals bend downwind and, therefore, you should generally look upwind from the clouds. As you drop from the middle altitudes, you should realize that generally high ground is better for thermal sources. When low, finding lift is a matter of identifying and utilizing thermal sources. Usually forest areas, woods, lakes, and such are not the best sources. Plowed areas, cultivated fields, and big paved areas are generally better. Towns or other areas that may have absorbed a lot of heat during the day are particularly good later in the afternoon. Big airport runways and interstate highways can be good sources. Oftentimes it takes a disturbance in an area where a good source may exist to trigger the thermal. For example, a truck on a superhighway can oftentimes kick off an excellent thermal.

Always watch for leaves rustling, which can be seen

easily because the backs of the leaves appear a much lighter color; and when the leaves are blown, you can see color changes in the trees. Grain or tall grass waving in a swirl in a cultivated field is an indication that a thermal is coming up from that spot. Small dust or trash devils, even in the eastern United States, are not uncommon and should be watched for.

The sunny side of hills and ridges are good thermal sources. Any terrain that catches the direct rays of the sun is likely to be better. It's better to stay on the upwind side when at or about ridge height level. Ridge lift is always a good possibility and has saved many a flight. If you have a ridge near your airport, it is excellent experience to prac- tice ridge soaring. If there is a soaring site with a ridge anywhere close to your area, it is worth the trip just to get ridge soaring experience.

Circling birds can be helpful in locating lift. Don't, how- ever, assume that all birds are brilliant or that they are climbing. They do sometimes circle in sink! They will suck you into the sink with them if you let them. Take care. However, if you are low and desperate, a hawk or a buzzard is a very good gamble. Remember that they can circle in a much smaller thermal than you, and you may not be able to stay with them down low. Soaring birds such as hawks and turkey buzzards have about the same sink rate and L/D at about 50 mph as a 1-34 or maybe a 1-26. They are, of course, more maneuverable and may be able to outclimb you. Any of the new glass ships can leave them at above about 50 or 60 mph when penetrating, in spite of their variable geometry wings. Most birds do not usually attack a sailplane unless it is close to their nest or in their restricted territory (e.g., eagles). The study of the realtionship between birds and soaring is much too broad a subject to cover here. We suggest you go to other references for more details of this fascinating subject.

Smoke is a soaring pilot's friend (assuming it's outside the cockpit). Always watch for smoke when you are in the middle altitudes and on the way down. This is for two reasons: Smoke is the best surface wind indicator and also represents a likely thermal source. Polluters of the atmosphere have at least one friend, the soaring pilot. Be on the lookout for smoke stacks and don't be afraid to thermal with your wing pointing right in the stack. However, you should be very conscious of the danger of fumes. These can be of any sort and can quite possibly be toxic. It is a good idea for a soaring pilot, when making a save over a smoke stack, to don his oxygen mask for a few minutes when circling in the smoke. Any time you don't feel well when circling in smoke, get out fast even if it means a landing. The toxic effect of industrial smoke can be a real danger.

Other types of smoke sources such as trash fires, brush fires, or forest fires should be watched for and utilized when possible.

Before we end this section a few general comments about flying low should be emphasized. Soaring is nice when you are high. The temperature is much lower, you are more comfortable, less anxious, etc. But when you get low, the temperature is much higher and just when the time arises that you should be able to concentrate most efficiently, you will be most uncomfortable and anxious. It all adds up to the fact that one is in a less safe condition when flying low. Therefore, a good pilot forces himself to be more conservative and more careful under these conditions. In summary: *The number one consideration, when down low, is landing safety; and locating lift is a poor second.*

5.10   HOW FAST?

Another important in-flight decision which causes a great
amount of difficulty and even more discussion is how fast
to fly between thermals. A whole science has grown up
around this subject and many theories are set forth from
which the pilot may choose. Most theories point toward
determining an optimum speed for maximizing overall cross
country speed. These are generally based on assumptions of
the ratio of up air to down air and are presented as speed
to fly vs. variometer reading, assuming that conditions
ahead will be the same as those just encountered. For the
serious pilot who is interested in the details and derivations
of these theories, we will give a few references here for
your further study:

1. Articles by Dick Johnson and Wil Schuemann in the
   Proceedings of the 1972 Symposium on Competitive
   Soaring, Soaring Symposia 1973.
2. Chapter 3 in New Soaring Pilot by Ann Welch,
   Lorne Welch and Frank Irving, John Murray Pub-
   lisher, 1968.
3. Article by Paul McCready in *Soaring Magazine*,
   January–February 1958.
4. Article by Weinberg in *Soaring Magazine*, June,
   1967, page 20.
5. Chapter 3 in *The Theory of Modern Cross Country
   Gliding* by Weinholtz, translation published in New
   Zealand, 1969.
6. Chapter 6 in *American Soaring Handbook* by Dick
   Johnson, published by SSA.
7. Chapter 28 in *Gliding* by Derek Piggott, Adam &
   Charles Black Publishers, London, 1958.

How much of the detail in these references should the

average non-technical cross country soaring pilot try to absorb and utilize? We feel that the serious pilot should be familiar with the McCready speed ring and if you cannot buy one for your sailplane-variometer combination, you should at least study the article by McCready or one of the other references fully enough to be able to construct a ring or table by yourself, or with the help of a technically-minded friend.

The speed-to-fly ring on your variometer is a great in-flight decision maker. You must make the decision as to how conservatively or how optimistically to set the ring, but once it is set the ring makes the speed-to-fly decision for you. Even a ring that may not fit the polar of the sailplane exactly is better than no ring at all. Just to indicate to you that our opinions are not unanimous, some of America's top soaring pilots do not even use a speed-to-fly ring. Dick Schreder, for example (who incidentally is a many-time U.S. National Champion), uses no ring but suggests a rather simple rule of thumb which you might like to consider. He says, "Fly with your variometer at a down setting equal to your last average climb rate." This means that you should adjust your speed so that the vario reads down to the same magnitude as its average up reading was during the last climb. If you leave a 300 ft./min. thermal, then adjust your speed so that your variometer reads 300 ft./min. down on the average. Another easy rule for pilots who fly club, rental, or other less sophisticatedly instrumented ships is to increase your speed to an average of about 20 percent greater than the best L/D speed. Faster than this would be called for in good conditions and slower in poor conditions.

Regardless of which rule or ring you use, your in-flight

decisions on speed should be tempered with good judg-ment, and in all cases you should speed up in sink and slow down in lift. This last statement sounds very simple, but it is one of the most difficult things for a new cross country pilot to learn. It is not so hard to slow up in lift, but forcing yourself to speed up in sink is difficult. This is necessary so that you decrease the amount of time you spend in bad air and increase the amount of time you spend in good air. This rule applies regardless of altitude; however, your average speed between thermals should be reduced with lower altitude.

When you reach an altitude where it is obvious you should accept any lift to prevent landing, your average speed should be reduced to best L/D speed to enable you to search the greatest area for lift. The whole game here is to increase the probability of finding lift. If this is not already an automatic reaction with you while soaring, then by all means remember this very important soaring axiom: *SPEED UP IN SINK—SLOW DOWN IN LIFT!*

5.11   ENTERING, CENTERING, AND LEAVING

It is not our intention here to go through a detailed analysis and procedure of exactly how a thermal should be flown. Most of the references listed in the previous section have chapters devoted to this subject. We don't hold much to the idea of memorizing rote procedures for centering in lift. Our discussion here will be more on basic philosophy, a few pertinent comments thereon, and a few hints which relate this subject to the aspects of cross country soaring.

Our philosophy is simple. First: Forget all the rote theories and procedures you have read about and think in terms of your mental picture of the size, shape, and location of the thermal and your position and heading in reference to this mental picture. We now assume that your manipulations of the controls are automatic and that you can keep the yaw string in the center without continual concentration. The only thing left for you to concentrate on is taking the feedback information that you get from looking outside and listening to your vario and using this information to vary your mental picture. You should update this mental picture all the time as to thermal size, shape, and location while varying your circle (position and heading) to coincide with it.

A few points of emphasis are in order. Never assume that the cross section of the thermal is circular or that its diameter is the same as the last one in which you flew. Another very, very common mistake in centering thermals is flying through the same bad air twice. Experienced pilots never cease to be amazed when beginners persist in doing this. It should be considered an unforgivable sin in soaring. To make the point even more strongly, we feel that each soaring pilot should be forced, at gun point, to sign a sworn statement saying that he hereby swears that he will never, ever, fly through the same bad air twice. Of course, if you are continually updating your mental picture as you should, you will have shifted your circle so that this would not ever happen to you. It *is* forgivable to fly through new bad air after revising your circle, but this soaring axiom is worth tattooing on some visible part of your body . . . *NEVER FLY THROUGH THE SAME BAD AIR TWICE!* A corollary to this might be that you should always fly through really good air as many times as possible and your changing mental picture should help you to do this.

Thermals may be oblong. There may be two or more

cores in close proximity and you should keep an open mind as to strange shapes. *Lift is where you find it.* Lift may be in long continuous lines and you may not need to circle to climb. This may be due to cloud streets (with or without the clouds), waves, ridge lift, etc.

If you are circling with another sailplane in the same thermal at the same altitude, watching him is often better than watching your vario. Of course, it is better if you are listening to your audio vario while you are watching him. Feedback from what is happening to his ship will help you to adjust your mental picture. It is quite noticeable, by watching him, when the "down" side of his (and your) circle occurs and when the "up" side occurs. This is valuable information to utilize.

Before leaving this topic, a word or two about entering and leaving thermals is in order. The answers were surprising to many pilots when the question of entrance procedure into a thermal was discussed at a symposium on competition soaring by several of the world's top soaring pilots. It was found that they each do it somewhat differently.

First we state the problem: You are penetrating at interthermal speed between thermals and you make the in-flight decision that you are at an altitude at which you feel you should take the next good thermal and climb back. What is your exact procedure? Do you slow down to thermaling speed at the first hint of lift on the vario? Do you fly all the way through the thermal and identify it before slowing down then turn around and come back and find it? Most of the more experienced pilots do not do much slowing down until they are sure that they are well into the core of the thermal.

Often there is heavy sink near the edges of a core and you want to keep your speed up through such areas. The direction you turn should not be determined until this time and the decision of which direction will be dependent upon which wing is kicked up the most or any other such evidence that makes you feel the thermal will be stronger one way or the other. The next step is a beautiful chandelle one way or the other and after one-half, or at most, one full turn, you should be stabilized at your thermaling speed in the proper configuration (flaps down perhaps) and exactly in the core. This little maneuver sounds easy; and if properly done, is one of the most exhilarating happenings in soaring. If you miss the core, and, believe me, we all do more than we like to admit, you will make the chandelle and slow down and watch to your horror as the vario sinks to the down side. Of the many frustrating experiences in soaring, this rates near the top and is unfortunately one of the most common and aggravating.

Perfecting this entering maneuver takes practice, practice, practice. It is difficult or impossible to consistently do this correctly without a well compensated total energy variometer system. Otherwise, the instant you begin to slow down, the vario will be lying to you. The absolute necessity for a well compensated system will be emphasized in later chapters. If you miss on the entering chandelle maneuver and find yourself at thermaling speed in sink, then you are faced with another of soaring's more agonizing decisions. What do you do now? Do you make another circle with a variation in the direction your mental picture tells you the thermal may be, or do you give up and drop the nose again and move on for a fresh try at a new thermal, having written off the valuable seconds that the frustrating sink circle has cost you? We wish we had some good specific advice to give for this common predicament. This is one of the places where soaring judgment built by experience must dictate your decision. We can add, however, that here is a good place to remember not to fly through the same bad air twice.

Leaving a thermal is usually not so difficult if the thermal is good, as it is likely to be when you have climbed up to where you are ready to leave, assuming that you have established yourself quite well in the core and are able to stay there. When you have decided to leave, first check for other ships at your altitude then make another circle during which time you build up your speed from thermaling speed to your interthermal speed or higher, and then when you are heading away from the direction which you want to go, tighten up your turn and cut back across the center of the thermal as you roll out on the departure heading, then leave the center of the thermal at your interthermal speed or higher. This is really a delightful maneuver and does not involve much of an in-flight decision once you have decided when to leave.

A much more common case of leaving a thermal is when the thermal seems to die out before you are as high as you feel you should be or if the thermal weakens appreciably for some unknown reason (which we all know is not infrequent!). In this case, the important in-flight decision is whether to try another circle with a variation or to move on. Unfortunately, there is no pat answer here either. This depends on the confidence you have in your mental picture of where the lift or core is. You will find many times that the lift defies figuring out and it is practically impossible to form an intelligent mental picture. Here again, your judgment and experience are the only things upon which you can rely in deciding to stay or to go. The higher you are, the more the tendency to go. The lower you are, the more the tendency should be to stay. One thing is for sure here. NEVER FLY THROUGH THE SAME BAD AIR TWICE!

5.12 GAGGLES

We will end this chapter with some additional comments about gaggles. We mentioned gaggles previously in relationship to finding lift, but here we would like to discuss some in-flight decision aspects of the actual flying techniques in gaggles.

It is not bad to fly with another sailplane at the same altitude in the same thermal, especially if you have an audio vario, but when you are at the same altitude in a thermal with three or more ships it is not only potentially dangerous, but you will not be doing your most efficient job of climbing. This is because your safety decisions dominate and you *must* keep track of *every* other sailplane at your altitude. Therefore, it is not good to fly in crowded gaggles if there is any other alternative. If you know and trust the other pilots, it is somewhat safer, but regardless of how well you know and respect the pilots, you should never let them out of your sight and never for one instant assume that they see you.

It goes without saying that it is unthinkable to fly extremely close to another aircraft if:

1.   You are very low, say below 1000 feet, or
2.   If you are not wearing a parachute.

Don't mix it up close unless you *KNOW* you can handle your ship perfectly at low speeds. Beginners often spend too much time staring at the vario rather than looking out. If there is any question in your mind about whether or not you have this habit, then make certain you break it before you fly in gaggles.

In overall summary it should be emphasized that the priority for in-flight decisions is unquestionably safety first. Maximizing speed and distance is an important but relatively poor second!

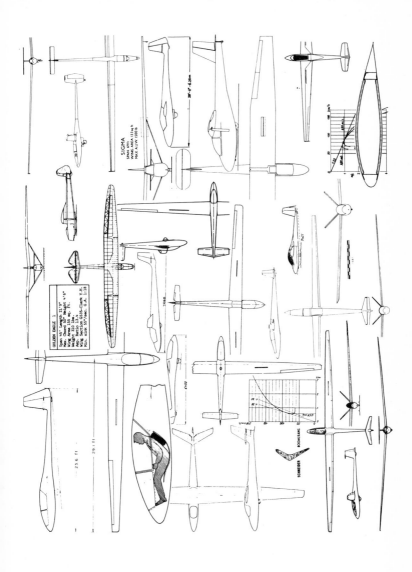

LANDING AWAY

6.1 INTRODUCTION

Since the emphasis and purpose of this text is to furnish useful information to pilots inexperienced in soaring cross country, the presumption of an off-airport landing should be accepted. Some experienced soaring pilots have flown a season or many contests without landing away from an airport, but not many! We might comment, they have missed meeting a lot of fine people and some pretty good farm hospitality by this excellent piloting. It is only logical to say that the pilot who is least efficient in cross country work is usually the most practiced at off-airport landings.

In Chapter 2 you found the recommended preparation for this event and now that you have become competent in landing in the simulated farm field, your confidence should be built to where you can begin to think about some of the other factors besides the actual safe landing technique.

6.2 REGARDING TERRAIN

Some of the suggestions in the earlier chapters are expanded and emphasized now. The planning of the flight should not be over bad terrain, but you do not always end up over the course you plotted. So, in flight, never head out on a course that will take you over terrain where you see that no good landing fields exist. Regardless of your height, you are in a machine that does not give you a chance for a "go around," or any alternative but to land if the weather should become unsoarable. Plan your flight over broad cultivated areas generally—not over vast wood-lands or rough mountains.

Above 3000 feet over this pleasant terrain, you can remain on course and proceed as described in the chapters on in-flight decisions, etc. Merely keep in range of generally hospitable country. When you reach 2000 feet above the ground and lift is less certain, begin to take closer note and work toward the area containing the better fields.

As your flight altitude approaches 1000 feet, begin to select the particular field that appears most safe. Check the surface wind, and make certain of its velocity and direc-tion. If you are in hilly country, better plan your pattern and concentrate on landing once you have descended below the 1000-foot level AGL. In the broad plains of the wheat lands, you can delay this final decision altitude to 500 feet. These heights are above the ground, of course, and must be judged from experience, for your altimeter setting will be inaccurate. The terrain elevation on the chart merely gives an approximation of the elevation of the field you have chosen.

6.3   FIELD SELECTION

Just because another glider is in the field *does not mean it is a good one!* When we laid out our simulated farm field, we picked 600 feet as an adequate sized patch in which to land; now when you are actually selecting a field, you will find most of them are far larger than this. Pick the most level field available with an absolutely even texture of bare earth. Priority in selecting the field should be in the following sequence of preference:

1. Plowed and harrowed. A plowed and harrowed field of even texture will have the least surprises. Surprises being large rocks, stumps, big holes caused by small animals. Your landing will probably cause little or no crop damage and, best of all, your ship will gently sink into the ground and stop quickly. Cattle, or other farm animals, will probably not be in the field to cause a problem after landing.

2. A field with a short new crop is a good second choice. The surface will still be visible, and the chance of cattle about the same as a newly harrowed field; but it will be a bit more firm as several weeks may have passed since plowing and the surface is beginning to pack and harden. You will damage these young shoots and the farmer may not be happy about this; but chances are they will recover and he may overlook the little damage your ship causes *if* you keep everyone behind the fence and out of his field. He could lose the whole crop to the trampling spectators.

3. Newly-mown fields are a third choice. The chances begin to increase because now you cannot see the actual ground and the even appearance of a newly-mown hayfield may be caused by the fact that the mower cuts the grain at an even height, though some of the stalks may be 20 inches from the bottom of the hole and the blade may have been set high enough to clear some rocks. Cattle may be let in to forage, so inspect this class of field extremely carefully while you are selecting it for a landing spot.

FIGURES 6.1 and 6.2 The same fields. Fig. 6.1 is taken from about 1800 feet over typical eastern U.S. terrain. Small but adequate fields with a wide variety of textures. Fig. 6.2 shows the same fields from just above pattern altitude. The overlay on Figure 6.1 is the author's opinion of the choice of landing fields. On Figure 6.2 it shows the pattern and final landing plan for either of two wind directions.

4. Pastures are normally very hard ground. The animals will have packed it in their grazing. If you must land in a pasture, pick an area with a very even appearance—flat with no small bushes (which hide rocks and holes). Cattle are probably around someplace. Look under the trees in the shade or down by the water. The farmer will probably not be particularly concerned about a pasture landing as long as

FIGURE 6.2 See caption Fig. 6.1

his cows aren't disturbed. He also will not care as much as you do about the damage you did to the ship on the hard landing or the damage caused by "Bossy" walking up your wing.

5. Landings in higher crops such as full-grown wheat, alfalfa, or even high corn *can* be made without serious damage to the ship or pilot. But your chances of damaging the ship by a hard ground loop are better than pretty good; a ground loop is almost a certainty. Crop damage could be enough that the farmer will ask for some reparations and retrieve becomes a real problem. In short, landing in high crops is very risky.

In the early spring at the beginning of the soaring season you will have more plowed and harrowed fields. As the season progresses and the crops grow, the availability of good fields decreases, and they tend to be mown hay fields. As the dry summer proceeds, cattle are let into marginal crops to forage because the pastures dry out. Late in the season as crops are cut the availability again increases.

The slope of a field is hard to judge from the air. Just remember if it appears to slope slightly from 2000 feet, it probably is too steep to consider as a first choice landing area. A cardinal rule to remember: Just as you land into the wind, land uphill. Land uphill even if you must land downwind. But, in rolling country where flat fields are rare and you are forced to choose between various sloping fields, pick a good one that has the least slope and the slope is up into the wind. Land into the wind and uphill.

Never land downhill is the rule to remember.

A sailplane is designed to fly at a very flat gradient. It does not require a very spectacular slope to fall away from your landing glider at a rate equal to or faster than its sink rate even with the airbrakes open.

6.4   PATTERN PLANNING

There is no such thing as bad luck in landing. If you have caused yourself some trouble in an off-field landing, don't blame anyone but yourself. There may be poor planning, or a poor approach, or a poor field, or a poor choice of a day for the trip, but Lady Luck cannot be used as a scapegoat for your poor judgment.

The classic wind indicators—smoke, blowing crops, etc.— disappear when you need them most, and when it comes to the first day to land away, you are over a number of fields

with no crops that are high enough to be blown. The
farmers aren't burning their barns so you are without anything but your memory of this classic adage—land into the
wind. What wind? Well, land into the prevailing wind—that
should not be so tough to remember. Didn't you pick a
downwind course to fly on this first try? How were you
drifting while you were thermaling? Since no other wind
indicators are present, use these for setting up the landing
pattern.

In addition to cattle, some other rather obvious landing
obstructions can reduce the number of good landing fields.
All good fields are surrounded by fences. Remember in our
training exercises we presumed this fact by clearing the
edge of the field while still well above fence height. Try to
plan your approaches so you are not even near a power
line. Do not plan to approach over any high obstacle—
especially one that contains high voltage; and do not plan
to roll under wires after landing. Presume that all tree lines
have hidden wires and that all roads are paralleled by
power lines—even farm roads.

The best advice is to land in the middle of a large field
and stop as soon as possible after touching down. Repeat:
STOP AS SOON AS POSSIBLE AFTER LANDING!

6.5 ACCESSIBILITY

The *last* consideration in selecting a field is the acces-
sibility for retrieving. You can carry the ship a long way in
a day or so, but it takes weeks to repair the damage done
in landing in a poor field. There are, however, a couple of
considerations to note if many good landing areas are
available. First, pick the good field nearest a paved second-
ary road. Try not to land just across a major river from

your crew or just across any major geographical barrier like a mountain. Landing on an interstate highway will result in a heavy fine. Do not even land nearby as you may be liable if you should cause an automobile accident by being an attractive hazard (that is, flying or landing close enough to a limited access highway to divert a driver's attention).

6.6 LANDING AND POST-FLIGHT CONSIDERATIONS

Airspeed control is the key to safe flying. Plan your pattern as you practiced back at your home field. Fly the full pattern and allow some extra altitude all the way around—allow for a good, clear, straight-in approach. Land in the middle of the best part of the field with plenty of height over any obstruction on final approach and lots of clear space ahead in case you overshoot.

Use full airbrakes and wheel brakes to stop as soon as possible after you touch down. You're subject to sailplane damage as long as you are moving on the ground, and you are damaging the field on which you are trespassing. For the sake of your sailplane and the farmer, stop as soon as you can after landing. You can push the glider a long way in a short time when compared to the time required to repair even light damage.

As soon as you have stopped and recognized that the flying portion of your flight is completed, take just a minute to relax and take account of things. Turn off your electric equipment—radios, varios, etc.—release your safety belt and chute harness. Then write down your landing time and turn off your barograph.

After you have had a drink of water and eaten some of the goodies, get out and take a look around for any unseen hazards such as cattle or horses or open gates from the pasture in the next field, then start to secure your ship. *If*

it is a calm afternoon, take your parachute and carefully
place it on the wing you have lowered into the direction
from which you think the wind may come. If it is gusty,
take out your tie-down kit and tie the ship down as securely
as you can. Leave your parachute in the ship and take out
your map, your SSA forms, and the jacket because it might
be some time before you return to the ship. But usually
about this time—ten minutes after you have landed—someone
will walk up—chances are it will be a boy or a young man,
if it is not the farmer. Now is the time to practice all the
charm you have accumulated, explain to your new-found
friend all about gliders; and if he appears a trustworthy
soul, appoint him guard over the sailplane while you seek
a telephone to call for your crew. Before leaving, close
the canopy and secure the sailplane and all its equipment,
instructing your newly-appointed security chief not to
allow anyone to touch the bird. Be sure to tell him your
name, where you came from and where you hope to find
a phone. Give him your business card and tell him it may
be an hour before you can return. If a large crowd is
present, ask a couple of these early friends to assist you
in moving *everyone* back of the fence, then have those
same guards prevent anyone from entering the field in
which you have landed. If possible, get help and move
the sailplane to the side of the field where it can be seen
without having the crowd walk on the field. Remember,
most of the damage to the farmer's property could be
caused by the commotion you have caused.

Regardless of the size of the crowd or the lack of a
single guard, you must be the one to go and call the crew.
Make the phone call yourself. Try to talk to your crew
personally even if it takes a few extra minutes. Before
calling get exact and detailed directions from the nearest

town to your landing site. Use your credit card and make it clear to the phone owner that the call will not be charged to his phone, and then give the following information to your crew:

1. The telephone number from which you are calling.
2. The name of the farmer or owner of the land where your ship is located.
3. Exact directions from the nearest town (that you are sure is on your crew's map) and the state or county road number nearest your location.
4. Coordinates of your landing point.
5. Assure them you are safe and the sailplane is secure. After completing your call, tell the owner of the phone your name (the business card is again very important) and that your crew may call back to recheck their directions. Ask this kind person to direct them to your sailplane.

6.7   FARMER-PILOT RELATIONS

Most farmers are not unhappy about the unannounced arrival of gliders. They are concerned about damage to their crops caused by the crowd the landing may attract; or if you have landed near livestock, they will be concerned about their welfare. Generally, they will be most congenial and friendly. To promote this attitude, act courteously and remember your position as an uninvited trespasser. Compliment him on the beauty of his field. Keep the crowds off his land. Do not present an affluent appearance; farmers are smart, they have to be to make a living today. If he asks you to pay for the damage and the trouble you have caused, he may ask for a considerable amount if you have appeared wealthy and ready to be plucked. If, on the other

hand, he feels he has gained a friend, he will allow you the
privileges he allows his other friends—that of hunting and
enjoying his "place." A few points of courtesy:

1. Always close the gates as you go from field to field.
2. Never climb over a wire fence if it can be avoided.
3. Never cut a fence (in Texas this is viewed with the
    same regard as cattle rustling).
4. Stay out of fields in which livestock are grazing, if
    at all possible.
5. Always locate the farmer or owner and tell him of
    your landing and identify yourself. If he is gone for
    the day, leave your card with your home address.
6. Keep, as part of your permanent records, the name

FIGURE 6.3   "I made it!" Silver badge distance without a scratch!

and address of the owner. Send him a Christmas
card.

6.8   WAITING FOR THE CREW

This seems to be a rather useless subject to consider, but
one of America's greatest soaring pilots has proven it to be
a subject worthy of serious consideration.

The day thus far has been extremely busy—so much so
that a series of check lists were used to make sure all
important steps and procedures were done in order. Now is
the first time you can feel free to relax and ponder.

After your phone call is completed and you are returning
to your ship, look at the sky and see if soarable conditions
still exist. If they do, why didn't you make your goal? If
they don't, what happened to your weather forecast? Consider carefully and write down some notes about what you
have learned.

Upon reaching the ship, relieve your guard after you
have given him the opportunity to sign your landing forms.
Pass the rest of your candy out to the kids and sell soaring
to the assembled multitude. No multitude? Or, maybe even
the farmer has left and you are standing alone in the
middle of the field? Good. Your crowd control problems
are solved and you can take a good look around and see
that the ship is safe and secured. If no livestock are around,
you can walk down by the road and sit down and write
your notes. Patience is a virtue that must be practiced—so
wait. Remember, your crew is as worried as you are about
getting to you so you must greet them when they come
driving up. Once you are together, don't forget to call back
and tell your telephone control that their duty day is
ended.

6.9 A FEW RULES FROM THE CHAPTER

Not in order of importance because they are all equally significant.

1. Never fly out over an area where you can't land safely.
2. Always land uphill.
3. Landing in high crops means a ground loop.
4. Never land on an expressway right of way.
5. Stop as soon as you land.
6. Fly a full pattern at normal speed and altitude.

CREWING

7.1 INTRODUCTION

The success of a cross country flight is dependent upon the efficiency of all of the components that make up the entire flight unit. These components consist not only of the pilot and his flight equipment, but also include his ground equipment, and, very importantly, his crew. The crew can be defined as the one or more persons who assist the pilot before the flight, at takeoff, during the flight, and in the retrieving. This chapter deals with the qualifications and duties of a crewman and also of the overall crew.

7.2 QUALIFICATIONS

Just as you carefully select the sailplane that you believe will carry you to your goal, your selection of a crew must be done with great discretion and judgment. The best crew chief for a married pilot is a wife who can drive with a trailer attached and will put up with the vile moods he will exhibit when he has not made his goal. A good, strong teenager who is enthralled with the very sight of a sailplane, can hold a heavy wing tip for ten minutes, and will accept your wife's commands tactfully, will complete an ideal crew.

Two people are sufficient; three, if one is a teeny bopper able to go for water when asked, and furnish sufficient diversion in moments of stress to relieve the tension without being a problem. But no more. Crewing requires decisions and action; therefore, the crew chief must decide and then do, so don't furnish enough extra minds to create a minority report. If extra hands are needed, there will usually be one or two around at the critical times of assembling and disassembling without hauling them for miles and miles of hot retrieve. It is becoming increasingly common for pilots of the new glass Standard Class ships to have only one crew member.

We will try to state more specific qualifications of a perfect crewman. This is something to shoot for and not something that you can expect to attain with every person from whom you solicit help.

Being a pilot is not in itself qualification enough to make a good crewman. It usually helps because familiarity with aircraft, and particularly sailplanes, is always an asset. Pilots generally have a better understanding of the needs of other pilots.

Do not assume that females never make good crew members. Actually they are not all bad, and sometimes can be very excellent. You bachelor sailplane pilots should concentrate your attention on the brainy and brawny broads. If brainy and brawny, they are more easily trainable. You married fellows whose wives do not fit these specs will have to suffer along. You girl pilots will have to interpret these suggestions as you see fit.

We seek here a person who is smart, stable, mature, alert, agile, reasonably muscular, and who is an excellent driver, map reader, etc. These are traits to look for with the hope of finding someone who has, at least, the majority of them.

One of the most, if not *the* most, important attribute a crewman can have, is the ability to get along and not to get on your nerves when you have had a bad flight. A pleasing, easygoing personality is to be cherished in a crewman. Sulky, temperamental people are best left at home, and this includes wives. This is particularly true during a contest when you must fly several days in succession. The lowest a human being can feel is after he's had a bad contest day in which he knows he has gathered few points. The good crewman must instill a spirit of competition and a desire to make a tremendous comeback the next day.

Be careful about choosing as a crewman an employer or anyone you cannot boss. Sometimes it is necessary to speak very directly with crewmen. A pilot must be concentrating on nothing but the flight and cannot even spare one second for the whims, feelings, or desires of the crewmen.

The following make poor crew for long retrieves: new female acquaintances, employees on their day off, friends who just came out to the field to watch, and anyone who has another serious hobby like golf. These are short in their understanding and patience and certainly not trained to disassemble at night in the rain with a cheerful countenance.

The common practice of two club members swapping days as crewmen, either for a contest or not for a contest, is an excellent idea. You should, however, try to choose club members who have as many good qualifications as possible and also a person for whom you would like to crew.

Hired crew (employees) are probably the best of any if they are well trained and capable and if you can afford it. Some of the better heeled top competition pilots have hired crew members at contests.

The question often arises: "Should I offer to pay a friend or acquaintance for crewing?" Crewing which is done at the home base by friends is not usually compensated. It is common practice, however, when crewing involves going to a contest away from home, for the pilot to pay the room and board as well as transportation for the crew during this period.

The following sections deal with what this well-qualified crewman whom you have chosen will be required to do.

7.3 TRAILER HANDLING

The biggest single job of a crewman is handling the sailplane trailer and automobile. You should not automatically expect an inexperienced crewman to know about such things. It is up to you to teach your crew (and yourself) to handle the trailer under all conditions. This means everything from high-speed driving to backing and parking. A good exercise (on an overcast weekend) is a trailer backing and parking contest for pilots and crewmen. It is really not a waste of time and can be very informative.

Be sure your crew knows all the specific details and eccentricities of your car and trailer rig. For instance, how to change the trailer tire as well as how to change the car tire. Are the jack and tools the same for the car as for the trailer? Do they know where the trailer jack is located?

It seems that no two trailers have the same light hookup details. Be sure your crew is familiar and be sure your system is foolproof. The same is true of the trailer coupler locking mechanism and the safety chain hookup details. If your automobile hitch and trailer have been designed for each other, this should be no problem; but many times when club equipment is being used, the automobile and trailer are not compatible. There is nothing more frustrating than trying to get a 1-7/8-inch coupler to go on a 2-inch ball when it is time to leave the field on a retrieve.

Is your car-trailer combination unstable at any speed with the trailer empty or loaded? Are there any special handling characteristics that your crewmen should know? What about the trailer brake system operation? For example, many trailers cannot be backed until someone locks out the brakes. It can really be a traumatic experience in the making if you fly off without telling a crewman about such a situation. Are there any special automobile fuel requirements?

These are a few of the items with which you should make certain that your crewmen are familiar. You should require a complete checkout with checklists. If an extended crewing period is coming up such as a regional or national contest, then this checkout procedure should certainly include practiced disassembly, even in the dark. You can help make this disassembly process easier by a little pre-season design improvement program on such things as loose trailer fittings, extra safety pins, etc. Keep the loose fittings to an absolute minimum and be sure they are properly stored. Safety pins are best put on a string or wire so that they can be undone, pulled out and dropped without being lost.

7.4   PREFLIGHT CONFERENCE

Even if your crew is for a one-flight deal, a preflight conference is a must. After the task has been chosen (or announced as in a contest), this preflight conference should include a dual study of previously prepared dual maps, including a discussion of the probable route and flight plan.

Decide *exactly* what your crew is to do if radio contact is lost. It is best to suggest that they continue to some specified place on your route, and hold. The specific location depends on the task. Have the crew call in every half hour after radio contact is lost. You might suggest they go to the approximate middle of a triangle or halfway up a leg if it is a goal and return task. They should wait on the highest spot in the vicinity.

During this conference, if not before, brief the crew carefully on the telephone call-in procedure. If it is not a contest flight, then you should also brief carefully the person tending the telephone. It is possible to use any manned phone (at home, at the airport, or even in another city). The procedure is this. The crew calls in, person to person, to the pilot. If the pilot has not been heard from, then the call is refused and there is no charge for the call. If the pilot has called in, then the call will be accepted and instructions given to the crew. The crew should always have pencil, paper, and maps ready when calling.

During this conference, you should also be sure that the crew has some cash. About half a day's wages is minimum. Also, he should have such things as your gas credit cards, telephone credit card number, car keys, trailer keys (the trailer spare or jack may be inside the trailer), car insurance information, car registration and title, ground radio license and instructions, and other specialized items that you might have. Always expect the worst to happen. If your crewman has a wreck, can he cope with the situation? How about a flat? Either on the car or the trailer? Can he take care of a speeding ticket or perhaps some simple mechanical trouble? How about radio trouble such as blown fuses, etc.? In general, you should not expect your crew to know as much about your car and rig as you do unless you have completely trained them.

If your crew, for example, is your wife and children, then it would not be cruel for you to test them (separately) on changing a tire (on car and trailer) at the start of a soaring season or, perhaps, any time you trade cars or trailer.

In summary, let's go over a sample checklist that you might use and add to for your crewmen. At least an hour before each flight (do not wait until takeoff time) you should go over such a list as this (add or delete items for your particular requirements):

1. Car keys
2. Trailer keys
3. Gas credit cards
4. Telephone credit card or number (write it down!)
5. Telephone number or numbers to call in (write it down!)
6. Car papers such as insurance, registration, title, etc.
7. Special gas, oil, tire pressure instructions, etc.
8. Special radio instructions
9. Road maps (folded and marked)
10. Sectional maps for crew (well marked)
11. Special radio codes
12. Cash for crew
13. Trailer hookup instructions (coupler, safety chains, lights, brakes, etc.)
14. Trailer spare tire, jack, and lug wrench location
15. Trailer papers (registration, title, etc.)
16. Radio check (two way)
17.
18.

7.5   RADIO PROCEDURES

Correct radio procedures are one of the most difficult things a soaring pilot, as well as his crew, must learn. Naturally, a beginning cross country pilot is nervous and excited and wants to share his experience with friends or crew on the ground. Unless you are the only one on 123.3, then keep your talk to a minimum. After your first few nervous flights, you should practice keeping quiet on the radio. *Nothing* makes you more unpopular at a contest or a busy soaring center than talking too much on the radio. All experienced cross country pilots will quickly attest to the fact that you cannot do a good job of flying a sailplane while talking on the radio, and anything that distracts from flying should be minimized, if not eliminated.

Radio talk should be absolutely limited to the briefest report possible. Generally, the pilot will want to simply let the crew know where he is and what he expects them to do. Here is an example of a typical report:

Pilot: Echo Delta

Crew: Echo Delta go

Pilot: Twenty miles—leg A—climbing—press (or: Twenty miles—Let A—low—hold)

Crew: Echo Delta roger

This report should be considered a maximum and anything in addition is absolutely superfluous.

When soaring on course, the pilot should keep the radio turned down or off. It seldom helps your flying listening to others. It's too distracting. The only time a pilot would leave the volume up is before going through a starting gate and maybe a little while after, if conditions are good. This is in order to check on the strategy of others.

The crew should *never ever* initiate a call to the pilot.

Their troubles are their own. The pilot has enough problems and should not be distracted.

Nothing brands you as an amateur quicker at a soaring site or in a contest than sloppy, careless radio procedure. When you go to a contest or anywhere around a soaring center, listen to the experts. You will notice that they are seldom heard. They are too busy flying. Remember, any time you touch the mike button, assume that you are speaking to a vast pilot-crew audience, not just to your crew. It seems that many pilots push the mike button and then try to decide what to say. Do not let this happen to you or your crew. You should think carefully what you want to say *before* pushing the mike button.

The crew should leave the radio volume full up at all times. The crew should *never* get out of earshot of the radio. A good crewman should be ready to grab the mike and answer on a two- or three-second notice when the pilot calls. This is a crewman's responsibility at all times during the flight until the pilot and crew are in visual contact on the ground.

When the crew is holding, they should always pick high ground, on the crest of a hill, for example. The radio reception is better at such a location. For this reason, the crew should not stop or slow down in low places or behind or between hills or ridges.

The crew should always be careful with high current drain radios. Do not leave the engine off too long unless you are sure of the battery condition. A good crew should always telephone back if they have not heard from the pilot in the past half hour.

A pilot, during the flight, should report to the crew about every twenty to thirty minutes, if possible.

7.6   WHEN TO LEAVE THE FIELD

The decision as to when the pilot should have the crew leave the airport is dictated by the role that they play in a possible relight procedure. A relight in a contest is when the pilot gets shot down very early or just after leaving the field and would like to have a quick retrieve back to the airport for a second assembly and start.

With this relight thought in mind, the pilot should have his crew leave the airport at about the same time that he does or maybe a little before. The crew should stick very close to the pilot at first, and be ready for a relight. The optimum condition is for the crew to keep the pilot in visual contact for as long as possible.

As soon as the crewman completes his wing running chore at takeoff, the crew should not stand around and watch the tow and have a social gathering with other crews. They should return to the car immediately to man the radio and the car and trailer should be hooked up, parked headed out, and ready to leave as soon as possible after takeoff.

It is especially important that the crew listen to the radio very carefully from takeoff until the pilot goes through the start gate. The ground radio should be in range of the ground start gate radio so that the crew can not only listen for the pilot to tell the start gate when he is going through, but they should also be able to hear the start gate tell the pilot whether or not he has had a good start. As mentioned before, the crew should not call the pilot. Wait until he calls you.

The crew and the pilot should not wait until after takeoff before thinking of getting the crew ready to go. It is a good idea, even before the sailplane is pulled out to the

FIGURE 7.1   Loyal crew at work!

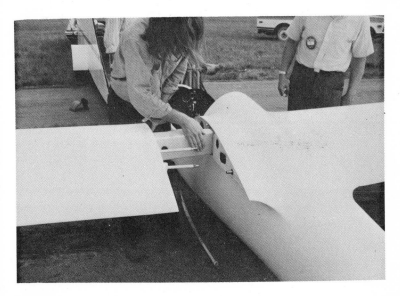

FIGURE 7.2   "Watch your fingers."

start line, to get the empty trailer completely secure, hooked up, and parked headed out. This is especially important at a contest.

7.7　RELIGHT PROCEDURE

Being able to get the pilot back for another start after a premature landing is the greatest test a crew can have. The pilot, however, should remember that he plays an important role in this procedure. After the pilot has landed and communicated with the crew by radio relay, visually, or by telephone, he should then determine the trailer route into the field and to the sailplane. He should get the ship to the side of the field next to the road, if time permits and if help is available. He should have the ship ready, untaped, fairings off, controls unhooked, etc. He should also have the sailplane positioned with respect to where the trailer will be so as to minimize the time required to get back on the road.

The pilot and the crew should, together, practice high-speed disassembly and assembly (but always with great care). You should *always* take time for a checklist for parts and trailer security before leaving a field after disassembly and also before takeoff after reassembly.

Remember, no amount of time saved is worth even a small ding or a small control not hooked up. There is a movement afoot to outlaw relights. The rules may reflect this before this book is printed.

7.8　NO-RADIO FLIGHTS

It is possible to complete many challenging cross country soaring flights of various lengths without the need for any radio, but this puts more of a burden on the crew and a rendezvous should not be expected as quickly. Tasks from your home base or even elsewhere are quite feasible without radio but it is certainly no longer recommended that you go to a sanctioned regional or any big contest without a good radio system. We suggest the following procedure for flights with no radio.

For short triangles or goal and return flights, say, of less than 200 kilometers, it is best for the crew to simply wait at the airport. For bigger triangles or goal and return, the crew should go to the middle of the task area and call in each half hour.

For free distance flights, the crew should try to average about 40 mph along the preselected route (usually downwind). If for some reason the flight is upwind, then, of course, the average speed should be slower. The crew should, again, call in every half hour, and this includes the first half hour.

Psychic crews have been known to be within 10 miles of the sailplane landing after a 200-mile flight, but this is a rarity.

7.9 PSYCHOLOGY

In summarizing this chapter on crewing, a few pertinent comments of a general nature are in order.

The training of the crew began when you started practicing for soaring cross country. On the days you went around the practice triangle, your faithful crew chief should be learning radio procedures and trailer handling. Most serious competition pilots have had the same crew chief for a long time and may have been together since the first contest. Crewing is a real art and a science, so you must develop someone to fill this required job as you become a cross country pilot.

A crew and each crewman must have a knack for developing rapport with the pilot. This is true whether it be a wife, girl friend, boy friend, employee, or whatever. They must be able to size up the pilot's personality and act accordingly. They must know when to keep their mouths shut. They must know how to handle a pilot after a very bad day.

A good crewman is: Where you want him, when you want him, and able to do what needs to be done— quickly, skillfully, and cheerfully!

CONTEST SOARING AND RECORDS

8.1 INTRODUCTION

This is the final stage of the disease. We started with landing in the little field and are working our way through to selecting the optimum sailplane for our use (and wallet). Now, we are going to discuss what you are going to do with this new talent you are acquiring. Not many competent cross country sailplane pilots can resist the lure of competition; and if they can, they are rare indeed if they do not, at least, try to win a state record.

8.2 COMPETENCY

You have to be good at soaring cross country to place in a contest. You can't win the day if you have not mastered the fundamentals of landing away and making in-flight decisions. You will learn more about these by participating in a contest than by any other means. Note the word *place* in the first sentence. You can enter if you are just learning, but you probably won't place. You should be competent to do the mechanics of soaring cross country and then soaring in contests will make you a master of the art.

Navigation becomes extremely important in soaring against time. Contest and record work are always a test of speed. Nothing destroys speed as fast as getting lost, unless you land away on a good day by making poor in-flight decisions.

Swinging the compass before a contest is a must. Rolling out of a thermal high in the haze on the proper track, and knowing exactly where you are despite the poor visibility gives you a big boost in time.

Leaving a weakening thermal before it quits when you have absorbed precisely the correct amount of its energy is a technique that championship pilots know, and to master this, you have to enter contests.

Advanced competition soaring is an art that requires practice as well as study. Nothing can beat flying cross country with another competition-minded colleague to get the required practice. And for study, note such articles as "Saving Seconds," by George Moffat, "Do's and Don'ts," by Dick Schreder and the "Philosophy of Winning," by A. J. Smith in the "Proceedings of the 1969 Symposium on Competitive Soaring." These gems reflect the wisdom that made the authors national champions.

8.3   WINNING RECORDS

The previous paragraphs give the impression that only an experienced sailplane pilot can make a name for himself in soaring. The list of State, National and World records do not, for some reason, bear this out. Many world records have been made by pilots relatively new to soaring. Certainly, they were very competent in the basics we have illustrated, but with not many years of soaring background.

Most State records are within reach of any serious cross country pilot and furnish good incentive to step out and try for a record.

The appendix includes rules and applications for state

records (SSA Item Number 3). This item is worth some study.

8.4   ENTERING A CONTEST

The Silver C distance leg is the standard criteria to qualify for entry in an SSA-sanctioned regional contest. As these contests grow in size, the enforcement of this rule becomes more necessary. Of course, many unsanctioned meets and camps offer excellent opportunities for the neophyte to gain experience and these normally have no experience requirements.

The pilot entry requirement to a national contest is a bit more complex, but the minimum is Gold C distance leg or high placement in a regional. Entry in any contest is normally made by writing to the club holding the contest at least a month in advance for information. You should receive by return mail an entry application stating the time, location, and entry requirements. Upon returning the application, you will receive the rules. *Read the rules.* Many contests are lost because the pilot made a mistake concerning the rules.

8.5   CONTEST TASKS

Today's higher performance sailplanes are beginning to make the free distance tasks obsolete so you can expect either goal and return or triangles to dominate the task selections. Usually the competition director likes to have at least one triangle of significant distance early in the contest, with a short goal and return for the last day so most of the pilots and crews can get started for home early. If he is a free distance advocate, he will usually call for this task on a day when the weather is forecast to be rather poor. And then, if no one goes far enough to call for a mandatory rest day, watch out for a fast short triangle the following day.

The "Cat's Cradle" or "Bikle Basket" are the unofficial more polite terms for "distance within a prescribed area." A task invented to give advocates of free distance an opportunity to do their thing without the possibility of a two-day retrieve. Few are really happy with this, but you might watch for it in the rules of any contest you enter. The idea is to fly any pattern within four or more designated points without ever retracing the course you have just flown. The speed advocates say it is just a botched up speed task and the distance people say it is too confining.

The discussions that accompany a goal and return of considerable distance on a poor day often follow the same lines of reasoning.

8.6   WHAT TO EXPECT WHEN YOU ENTER

Regional contests are of five days duration and require three days of contest flights to be called a contest. Sometimes the five days may be on two weekends, but more often they will be five straight days. Usually the two days previous to the official contest date are practice days. At well-run regional contests, the practice day preceding the contest is just like a contest day to iron out the bugs in the operation and to give everyone a chance to familiarize himself with the terrain and the contest site.

A typical regional contest day will begin with a pilot's meeting around 9:30 to 10:00 a.m. Take your crew chief and the charts and be on time, for nothing is repeated for the benefit of late comers. The competition has begun and you can't rely on any advice from the more fierce members of the sport. The contest manager will introduce the various dignitaries, such as the chief scorer, the line chief, the meteorologist, the competition committee and the competition director. The chief scorer will make some threatening remarks to those pilots who fail to turn in landing cards or whose coordinates are in gross error. The line chief will do the same regarding pilots and crews who fail to observe rules regarding cars on the flight line and those who fail to be in the takeoff lineup on time.

The competition director will then give a short lecture about rules and procedures and announce the task for the day and review the turnpoints. After the moans or cheers of the contestants, he will give the times of the opening and closing of the takeoff line, the start line and the finish line.

The weatherman will follow with all the data he has available and will make a few excuses about lack of upper air soundings or give some other reason so he can weasel out of any criticism if the day turns out different from his forecast.

Usually, he will close his lecture by a sincere request for data from the returning pilots regarding conditions actually encountered on course. This last request will go unheeded by the pilots, generally, which shows what selfish people competition pilots really are when in heat.

After the piercing questions addressed to the "met" man are successfully fended off, a procedure of extreme seriousness begins which will really have a rather small bearing on the outcome of the contest. This ritual is the drawing and selection of takeoff times. Each pilot draws a number from a hat which tells the order of his opportunity to select the takeoff time he prefers. Takeoffs are usually scheduled at one-minute intervals, so the takeoff board is marked with pegs for each minute after the takeoff line is opened. As your turn to select comes up, you should carefully review the weather conditions and cast an eye on the time selected by the pilots you think may win and then with the sure voice of a confirmed crap shooter, pick the time on the earlier side of the prime takeoff hour.

This completes about 45 minutes; and if the meeting began at 9:30, it is now 10:15 and the takeoff line may start at '11:30. The line chief requested all sailplanes to be in the takeoff lineup twenty minutes before the takeoff time selected and you can plan on taking, at least, 15 minutes to be in position if your tie-down area is within a hundred yards of the line. So there is very little time to rest between the end of the pilots' meeting and launch. As mentioned earlier, get a good breakfast, for it will be a long time before you sit down to eat again. Better take a sandwich and some Gatorade to the flight line to have before takeoff.

This is when the various check lists and good crew coordination really count. All of that practice in assembling and getting ready to go for each of your noncontest cross country flights really pays off during this crunch.

If you are really serious about winning, remember you can adjust your takeoff time at any time before you actually go by going to the board (which should be near the flight line) as the takeoff time approaches and moving your card to any empty peg. This ploy is used by experienced pilots to attempt to fake out their opponents by last-minute jockeying—especially on days when conditions are poor and there is a good chance the whole show will be to no avail anyway.

The real time that counts is when you go through the start gate on speed task days.

8.7   THE STARTING GATE

This invisible area of sky extends from the surface to 1000 meters (3300 feet) in the air and is 1000 meters wide. Usually, the start line on the ground is a portion of runway or road with the timing tent at one end and a large marker at the other. The height is measured optically by an observer located at some distance 90° to this line who watches through a series of frames. If you appear to be within the frame when you cross the start line, you have a "good start" and this fact is normally transmitted on the radio immediately.

A few tips to the beginner. You can go through the start gate as many times as you wish. If you go through at red line airspeed at the very top of the frame and then pull up to your best glide speed, you have gone through the gate in a most efficient manner. Should you then encounter a thermal of excellent strength to a good altitude, you are off to a really "good start." If, however, after this blazing start you encounter a dead area of frightening breadth, you may work anything you can to get back up and return to blast through the gate again taking care, of course, to remember that the rest of the course must be flown and you cannot continue this courting procedure indefinitely, but must commit yourself to go at the most opportune time of day to fly the course.

The competition director will give a warning about traffic through the gate and mention that he cannot accept a rate of more than one every thirty seconds so you must use care about watching out for others who are going through at the same time.

Also, quite naturally, thermaling in the vicinity of the gate is dangerous and you will be embarrassed by being scolded at the next morning's pilots' meeting for this fool-ish error. Care must also be taken about your speed exceed-ing the red line on this pass. There is a tendency to push to the limit if a little high and if the day is gusty, you could easily exceed the design strength limit of the ship.

8.8   HOW MUCH DOES IT COST?

Section 4 of Chapter 1 lightly speaks of the cost of soaring and implies that the top competition pilot has a considerable investment in his fully-equipped sailplane kit. He does, but the 1-26 pilot who enters a club ship in the SSA sanctioned regional or local 1-26 contest also must be ready to meet some expenses.

A five-day contest means a minimum of four nights in a motel at $15.00 per person plus meals for the pilot and crew and about 1200 miles on the car. It looks about like this:

Motel $15 × 4	—	$ 60
Meals $12 × 4	—	48
1200 miles @ 12¢	—	144
2 extra tows @ $6	—	12
Entry Fee	—	50
		$314
Plus Contingency and miscellaneous		$ 36
		$350

Some pilots beat this figure somewhat by camping on the airport.

So it is about $350 for a five-day meet plus your fixed annual expenses of about $100 for liability insurance and some extra maintenance on your trailer, ship and instruments of about $50 annually. Therefore, a season of soaring cross country with two regional contests plus some record attempts would add up approximately like this:

2 Regionals @ $350	$700
5 Cross countries @ $25 each	125
Liability Insurance	100
Miscellaneous maintenance	50
	$975

Roughly, a budget of $1000 a year not counting depreciation on the equipment.

The very first words of this chapter stated that competition soaring is the final stage of the disease; and if you ask most any pilot who flies in national contests about the total cost of his hobby, he will say it costs more than he will admit to himself, but he is hooked on the habit and spends every cent he has to try to win. If he has any money left over, he is probably hiding it to buy a later model super sailplane. A wife who crews and helps to pinch pennies to support such a devotee is to be cherished and cared for above all other considerations.

8.9   COMPETITION AND RECORD-MAKING EQUIPMENT

Since the object of a record-breaking flight or of competition is to be better than all others, all of your equipment must operate exactly as it was designed to operate throughout the flight. Therefore, it must be in excellent condition. Instruments, radios and personal gear must be absolutely dependable.

Instrument mounting and plumbing must be well designed and able to withstand the heavy vibration of long-distance trailering.

The barograph and batteries are probably the two most abused and poorly mounted items in the sailplane. These always seem to be tucked away in some last-minute rig that would make a good aircraft mechanic turn grey. A barograph and the electronic gear the batteries drive are expensive necessary items and as such deserve better treatment. A variometer that sticks is useless, as is a total energy compensating gadget that doesn't work. Many PZL compensators are mounted in reverse in American sailplanes because the Polish word for pitot begins with a C so the fellows hook it to the capacity, which is just reverse. Read carefully Chapter 9 regarding the proper method and design of instrument plumbing.

Carefully cover your pitot and static ports while trailering. You won't know for sure that all of your instruments are working until you are in flight, so protect them all the time; and if you have them mounted securely with all lines neatly fastened down, they are more likely to be dependable.

8.10   RADIOS

Radios are viewed by some as having no place in such a pure thing as a sailplane, but these classic souls are coming around to seeing that good communication can save miles and miles of needless driving by the retrieve crew; therefore, hours of time wasted waiting. The capability of a 38 to 1 sailplane to cover extended miles on a record attempt makes the retrieve crew drive hard and fast to hope to be near when it lands after a long flight. When the pilot alters his course to use the changing weather pattern, the crew must know or they may be a hundred or more miles from the final landing point at the end of the flight.

Good communications between crew and pilot in contests save hundreds of miles of needless driving. Many pilots have their crews merely drive to a point just outside the airport on a rise along a good road and hold for short triangle or goal and return flights. They depend on radio relay to the sailplane if it should go down.

If the day is good, a sailplane can usually stay high enough to communicate with the crew throughout the flight.

The dependability of ground and air radios is of great importance for nothing frustrates and irritates like intermittent incomplete communications unless, perhaps, it's the thought of $1000 invested in equipment that won't work when you need it.

8.11 YOU CAN ENTER AND WIN

The big "if" in any sport is the desire of the participant to win. If you want to win soaring contests and break records, you can. You must practice and become competent and try harder than anyone else.

Practice means 150 hours of cross country flight per year after your first year of 300 hours. George Moffat flies at least this number of hours and doesn't count flights of less than fifty miles! A. J. Smith and Dick Schreder took one summer and flew every spare day cross country in competition against each other!

Read the many fine books and articles by champions such as the *American Soaring Handbook* and *The Proceedings of the Symposia on Competitive Soaring* in which they reveal their secrets.

Finally, with practice to gain competence, you can win—*if you want to!*

PHOTO IDENTIFICATION

EVENT	TIME	FRAME NO. Cam. 1	Cam. 2

1

SSA-SANCTIONED
SOARING CONTEST

PILOT'S TURN POINT & LANDING CARD

PILOT'S NAME_____

DATE_____

CONTEST NO._____

H.Q. PHONE NO._____

FOLD LINE

Pilot must phone Headquarters as
soon as possible after landing
even if he is in contact with his
crew. Score will not be counted
unless this card, properly filled
out and signed, is received by
scorer prior to announced deadline.

I certify that all information
on this card is correct.

_____
Pilot's Signature

-24-   SSA Form SR-6

FIGURE 8.1(a)   SSA Official Landing Card (front).

2

LOCATION OF LANDING

Make sketch for all landings
made off airports shown on
Sectional maps. Show nearby
roads and towns with distances
required by scorer

Lat._____ ° ' "

Long._____ ° ' "

↑ N

Crew instructions:

Fill in card completely before
telephoning headquarters.

3

LANDING CERTIFICATE

I (we) certify that sailplane
No._____ did land at the place
described to the left at approxi-
mately_____(time)
on_____(date).

WITNESS
#1 Name_____

   Address:_____

   City_____

   Phone_____

FOLD LINE

#2 Name_____

   Address_____

   City_____

   Phone_____

Phone where pilot may
be reached:_____
Approx. dist. flown:_____
Turn points reached, in sequence,
by number:_____

FIGURE 8.1(b)   SSA Official Landing Card (back).

INSTRUMENTS AND EQUIPMENT

9.1 INTRODUCTION

Soaring, like almost any other sport, has a great variety of equipment and instruments which vary widely in cost as well as usefulness. The most sophisticated of these can tax the pocketbook of any enthusiast.

We will try to outline in this chapter priorities on instruments and equipment for limited budgets. Details and theory of how they work will not be covered except maybe in a few simple, but important, instances. Information on where instruments and equipment can be obtained will be avoided except in isolated cases. There are several major suppliers in the United States and these distributors are profuse in their advertising in *Soaring*. We will try to give you information that will enable you to select your equipment intelligently.

A sailplane without any instruments is considered pretty useless as well as illegal. A sailplane plus its instruments is an overall system and should be considered as such. The degree of sophistication of the system should meet the needs of the pilot and his anticipated tasks. An average cross country soaring machine will include, in addition to basic flight instruments, at least two variometer systems and probably a radio, barograph, parachute, computer, and other personal equipment. These are the types of items covered in the following articles.

9.2   VARIOMETER SYSTEMS

A variometer is an instrument that tells the rate at which you are going up or down. If you are a power pilot, you might think of it as a very sensitive rate of climb instrument. There may be a few training sailplanes around that do not have any variometers, but one should not consider cross country flights until he is familiar with a sailplane with good variometers. Seat-of-the-pants flying with no variometers is just not good enough to allow efficient climb capability in thermals. Since this instrument is so vital to soaring, this is one case where we will explain the operating principle in simple terms. More details can be found in advanced references.

All variometers in sailplanes today work because the higher you go the thinner the air becomes and, therefore, the lower the air pressure. We do not mean that you have to go up several hundred feet to be able to measure a pressure difference. Suppose you pick a small box from the floor and set it on a table with a normal motion. If a good, modern, high-response vario were mounted in the box, you could make its needle peg in this pickup motion. This may be a faster response rate than you would need, but it shows the great sensitivity available in sailplane instrumentation today. Usually the heart of a variometer system is the reference chamber, which is an insulated enclosure of plain old air. As you move this reference chamber up, the air outside the chamber is thinner, and has less pressure, than that inside the chamber and, therefore, some of the air inside the chamber flows out. This chamber is often nothing more than a thermos jar. Measuring the very small amount of flow that comes out of such a container is the whole "trick" of the variometer.

If the reference chamber, which is fixed inside the sailplane, goes down instead of up, then the reverse happens and there is a small amount of flow into the chamber. Older type instruments measured this flow with pellets, as indicated in Fig. 9.1. Later models, many of which are still in common use, use the mechanical vane arrangement in Fig. 9.2. In most of the latest electric variometers, this small flow in and out of the reference chamber cools a pair of small thermistor beads differentially. These thermistors are in an electrical bridge circuit, the output of which is amplified and drives a meter whose reading is proportional to the flow which is, indeed, proportional to the up rate or down

PELLET TYPE

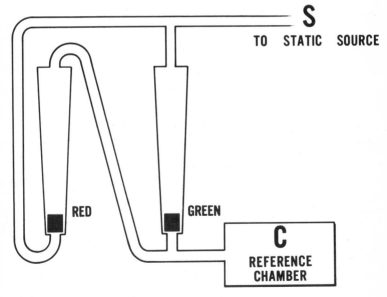

FIGURE 9.1

VANE TYPE

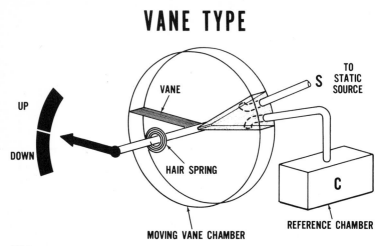

FIGURE 9.2

rate of the sailplane. Fig. 9.3 is a common arrangement of this electric thermistor type variometer.

A variometer, as described above, will respond any time the sailplane goes up or down due to any cause. If you were in absolutely still air and you dived down at 100 mph and then pulled up abruptly, the variometer would indicate a down during the dive and a violent up during your abrupt pull-up. Variometer readings which show up due to this changing of speed are called stick thermals and are readings which are strictly a result of your going up due to loss of speed and not because the air is taking you up. It is essential in efficient cross country soaring to be able to rid ourselves of variometer signals which are due to changes in speed or changes in energy due to changes in speed of the sailplane. We need to have a signal that will be proportional to this energy change due to speed change which can be used to cancel out part of the total flow signal from the

THERMISTOR TYPE

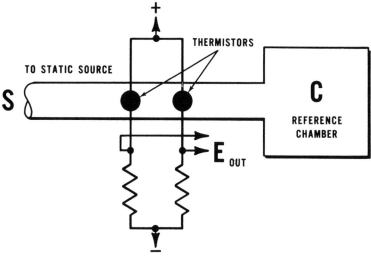

FIGURE 9.3

reference chamber. The net signal will hopefully be due only to the sailplane going up in rising air. The arrangement in Fig. 9.4 shows how we can get a net flow to our vario indicator from the reference chamber which has the undesirable stick thermal part canceled out.

One method of total energy correction is the use of a diaphragm-type compensator placed in the line from the pitot to the line coming from the reference chamber. The deflection of this diaphragm is proportional to speed change effects on the pitot pressure and it pulses just enough flow into the indicator line to take out the undesirable part. If the system is adjusted properly, then the indicator only indicates that the sailplane is going up due to rising air and not due to speed change. The restrictors

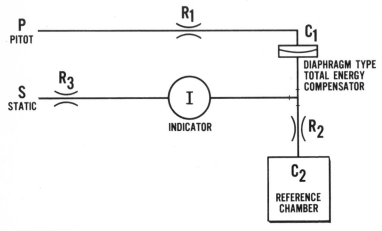

FIGURE 9.4

R_1, R_2, and R_3 are put in the system to adjust the
response speed of the instrument and will not be discussed
here. A more detailed discussion of this vital subject of
total energy compensation can be found in the articles by
Mr. Gene Moore in the *Proceedings of the First Annual
Symposium on Competitive Soaring* (1969) and the *Proceedings of the 1970 Symposium on Competitive Soaring*
published by Soaring Symposia.

Another method of total energy compensation is with
the use of a small venturi tube in the air stream which also
gives a pressure signal proportional to speed. This pressure
is also plumbed into the system to cancel the unwanted
part of the total signal. These devices were popular before
the advent of diaphragms but lost favor in recent years. It
is interesting to note that they are gaining popularity again.
A new smaller, lower drag design is now available (research
paper on this device was presented at the XII OSTIV

Congress, Alpine, Texas, 1970, and published in *Sailplane and Gliding*, Dec. '70–Jan '71, page 453). This venturi is simpler and easier to adjust than the diaphragm but it must be mounted in the air stream and, therefore, results in more drag.

The importance of having a good, well-adjusted total energy variometer system cannot be overemphasized. This is an absolute "must" for efficient cross country soaring. Do not pay any attention when pilots start talking about the virtues of one brand of variometer vs. the other brand of variometer. In general, you should know that all variometers of recent manufacture are generally very good; what makes them bad is being in a bad system. The system includes the static source, diaphragm, reference chamber, restrictors, as well as the indicator. If the system does not work, it is common practice to blame the manufacturer of the indicator, but this is quite often not the trouble. If you intend to purchase and install your own system, you should get Gene Moore's articles and study them very, very carefully.

Electric variometers are popular because they commonly have an audio attachment which gives forth an audible sound whose pitch changes in proportion to the meter reading, or in proportion to how much you are going up. Many pilots feel that this is not just a luxury but is a necessity because it enables them to "read" their variometer while looking outside at other sailplanes.

Another big advantage of electric variometers is the fact that they usually have scales for strong and weak conditions. An audio attachment for nonelectric variometers is now available and is proving to be quite popular. Electric variometers cost $200 to $300, whereas a good vane-type mechanical variometer such as the PZL or the Winter can be had for about $75. A diaphragm-type total energy compensator can be bought for about $25, and the audio (PIEP) for nonelectric variometers is about $90. The Moore (no longer available for sale), the Cambridge, and the Ball are the most popular American-made electric variometers, while the English Crossfell, the German BSW, Westerborer VW5KB (with electric compensation for $500), and Hornig are among the most popular European electrics. All of these instruments are good, and you should not blame them if your "system" is screwed up.

Special super varios with built-in computers are coming on the market. They display not only vertical speed but average climb over various times, descent speeds, optimum speed to fly, a zero "reader" (which when kept centered will result in the glider being flown at an air speed automatically calculated to produce the best overall cross-country speed), and many other electronic wonders. Unfortunately, the high price ($700 to $1000), difficulty to adjust, and lack of reliability have slowed general acceptance. Time, we feel, will cure these troubles, and these and other more sophisticated instruments are coming. The two we have seen so far are the Skye-Air Data Computer Mk. 2 from England and the Pirat from Switzerland.

9.3   OTHER BASIC FLIGHT INSTRUMENTS

Although we will not be watching them nearly so carefully nor often as the variometer, we do need a few other basic flight instruments. The first are the airspeed indicator and the altimeter. The altimeter is the same as in any power plane and almost any sensitive altimeter is satisfactory. Since you will not be doing much instrument flying, you probably will not "set" the altimeter nearly so often as in power flying; it is even satisfactory to buy surplus English instruments with milibar settings for pressure. This is an inexpensive solution to the altimeter problem. Surplus altimeters can be had for less than $75. New American altimeters are more like $100 to $200.

Some airspeed indicators in slower-speed power aircraft are satisfactory for sailplanes, but since this is not a particularly expensive instrument, it is better to have the best. A good helicopter airspeed indicator that makes 1½ revolutions to 150 mph is in common use and costs less than $100. It is desirable to have an airspeed that is very sensitive and has big graduations in the thermaling speed range. We prefer one, for example, that has a division mark for each mile per hour or knot in the 35-to-55-mph range. Imported PZL or Winter indicators of this type cost about $50 to $75 and are excellent.

Many different type compasses are in use in sailplanes. The 2¼ inch such as the Air Path C2300 are common and cost about $20. With the rapid turning of sailplanes, these compasses are not particularly well damped. The German 2¼-inch Ludolph is in common use for about $75. For instrument flying where you would like to roll out on a heading, the English Cook compass is excellent and is in common use. The Cook must be mounted away from the panel and may be a bit of a problem in this respect. Care should be taken to mount the compass as far away from an electric variometer as possible since the meter of the vario contains a magnet. It is also good practice to keep the compass as far away from the radio as possible. The compass should be swung as in a power plane and a correction card installed if necessary.

Since gyros are banned from soaring contests in the United States and there is very little other instrument flying in sailplanes in the U.S., we will minimize our discussion on gyros. Most ex-power pilots are uncomfortable without at least some sort of a gyro, so quite often you see the Mitchell pictorial turn rate indicator in cockpits. This is a satisfactory instrument. Also common are the German Gauting 2¼ in. diameter, 4½ volt, 1 min. turn, turn and bank instrument. For pilots who feel the need for an artificial horizon, the Bendix J8 with a transistorized power supply driven by a 14-volt source is popular.

9.4   RADIOS

When considering sailplane radios, the first thought is how much power is required because we do not carry alternators, generators, or gigantic batteries. Most sailplane pilots today insist on a crystal controlled receiver; however, the Mentor tunable receiver is proving quite popular. The cross country soaring pilot sometimes needs to contact flight service stations, control towers, unicoms, etc., and therefore having extra channels is a convenience.

The Bayside has been the standard radio in soaring for many years, but this company is no longer in business and new Baysides are not available. The Bayside is unbeatable from a current drain standpoint and requires the minimum in batteries. The BEI 990 (90 channel Bayside) is the most popular airborne set. The BEI 901 (single channel—sometimes modified to two channel) is a popular ground (car) set. The dash 1 (one watt) and dash 5 (5 watt) seem about the same in output and many pilots still swear by the one watt Bayside.

Many new solid state radios are now available in many models. Previous editions of this text included a table listing model, channels, watts output, power required (amps), weight and cost. The scene changes too quickly in this relatively unstable market to keep such a table up to date. We recommend, if you are in the market for a sailplane radio, that you prepare such a table. Talk to all the unbiased experts you can find. Collect all the brochures but be sure to read the fine print on the back under specifications, especially the power drain, weight, etc. Each pilot must weigh the features he considers most important and work up some kind of formula which includes cost, weight, power required, power output, number of channels, etc.

Among the most popular radios now are the Bayside, Bendix RT221B, Bertea ML-200, Dynair SKY-515A, Genave Alpha 10 and Alpha 100, Mentor, and Radair 10S. You pays your money and you takes your choice. We suggest you shop for "deals" and discounts. You can get discounts up to 1/3 off list on some radios, but this may or may not be a good deal. Who do you send it to if it quits? Who installs? Is the warranty good if you install? It's often less expensive in the long run to pay a little more initially and buy from a reputable dealer that you know and trust.

The above radios are for the glider. What about for the crew car on the ground? It is much better to have two or three channels so that if one gets crowded with too much talk, it is possible to communicate on other channels. Since the automobile battery is available, there is less worry about power drain, however, it is still nice not to have to keep the automobile running while the crew is waiting with the radio on. Most of the above manufacturers make a set which is packaged in a portable box complete with batteries, loud speaker, etc. This package usually costs about 25% above the basic radio cost. Some pilots use as ground stations, obsolete powered aircraft radios such as the King

KX90, Narco MK12, Collins, etc. The legality of these multi-channel sets is questionable. A license is required for the legal operation of the ground station in the crew car. It is hard to say what percentage of the pilots operate these sets completely legally.

The best antennas for ground stations are the specially tuned, bumper mounted rigs with loading coil sold by Rainco, Graham Thomson Ltd., and others, for about $50. The airborne antenna is usually built into the sailplane. Most of the new fiberglass ships have a quarter wave antenna mounted in the vertical fin with an adjustable antenna coil which is accessible through a small hole. Careful attention to the antenna systems can greatly improve communications between pilot and crew.

9.5   BATTERIES

Batteries are generally conceded to be the best way to store the power that must be taken along to drive sailplane instruments. The power is usually needed only for the radio and the electric vario; but if gyros are installed, then extra power is required. The problem is to find the most power for the least amount of weight. Cost is also important and most sailplane pilots have taken to the new developments in rechargeable batteries in an attempt to gain the most amp-hours per pound per dollar.

Regular dry cell batteries are still in limited use, but they are giving way rapidly to the rechargeables. Most radios and some instruments require 12 to 15 volts D.C.

Nickel cadmium (Ni-Cads) are fairly common, very satis-factory, but very expensive new. These can often be found government surplus for a reasonable price. Many pilots use 12 of the type AH6R (1.2 volt per cell) taped together and wired in series to give 15 volts. These cells can be had from Esse Radio Company, 368 South Meridian Street, Indianapolis, Indiana 46225, for $2.95 per cell. Less expensive and in common use are pairs of the 7½ volt Eveready No. 560 alkaline rechargeable batteries. Also popular are the sealed lead-acid Globe gell-cell packs sold by several distributors of sailplane equipment and elsewhere.

Batteries must be mounted so that they can be removed for replacement or recharging and this often gives rise to slipshod installations. Great care should be taken with installation of batteries because they are quite heavy and can wreak havoc in rough air if they break loose.

9.6   OXYGEN SYSTEMS

Not all sailplanes need oxygen systems. Those who fly in high terrain where cloud bases are commonly above 10,000 feet msl, have need for oxygen as do those who fly in any area where wave flying is anticipated.

For high thermal flying almost anywhere, excluding inside of clouds, and for even wave flying in the East, a continuous flow system is quite satisfactory. The common bottle size in most sailplanes in the 22 cu. ft. bottle which sells for about $50. Oftentimes a smaller bottle is used and once in a great while you see a larger bottle in some sailplanes. For the simple continuous flow system, a simple but good $10 mask is OK. For high wave flying, above 20,000 feet, it is *absolutely imperative* that a pilot get thorough and careful training and talk with experienced experts about specialized equipment. Since this is not ordinarily encountered in cross country soaring, we will not pursue the matter here.

A very strong recommendation is never to buy used oxygen equipment and forget about trying to find surplus oxygen equipment unless you are a real expert.

In cross country soaring, oxygen should be used at
10,000 feet during cross country soaring because this is a
stay at 15,000 feet for an hour or more with no oxygen,
but we are recommending some oxygen periodically at
10,000 feet during cross country soaring because this is a
physiologically demanding sport and this use of oxygen will
ensure peak efficiency.

For the same reason, we recommend going on oxygen
for at least ten minutes before an anticipated landing or at
any time later in the day when you feel tired and run
down. We also highly recommend that all pilots who anticipate any high altitude flying should take the military
physiological training course available to SSA members (in
some parts of the country).

9.7 PARACHUTES

The standard parachute for glider pilots is a thinly
packed, quick-opening back pack with quick fit ejector
snaps on the harness. The canopy is usually 26 or 28 feet
and the whole rig usually weighs about 18 pounds. There
are a few very special chutes, some chest packs and some
special compartment packs, but the majority are the back
pack mentioned above. The more expensive ($385) steer-
able Security parachute is, however, increasing in popularity. It is recommended that anyone anticipating the
purchase of a parachute for cross country soaring should
read the article on this subject in the November, 1969
Soaring.

Pilots flying in the desert regions in high temperatures or
at high elevations fields should consider a larger (or slower
descent) chute. Density altitude does influence chute
descent rate and can become an important survival factor.

One last note on parachutes. Between us we have gotten out of sailplanes (on the ground) thousands of times. Always the same way! Open canopy, undo safety belt and shoulder harness, unclip parachute, climb out. We have done this so often that it dawned on us, and fear struck ... if we ever had to jump, we would probably go through the same automatic sequence including the unclip parachute step. We are now on a crusade to encourage everyone to practice (at least several times a season) getting out of the sailplane with the parachute on! Maybe it would be good practice always.

9.8 BAROGRAPHS

All cross country soaring pilots should own or have access to a barograph. A barograph is simply an instrument which makes a permanent record of altitude vs. time. The time scale is usually the rotation of a drum driven by a mechanical clock mechanism. The vertical altitude scale is driven by a pressure measuring barometer, the guts of which are essentially the same as an altimeter. The record is usually on paper and is permanent so that it can be removed for study or for verification of the flight.

Barographs for FAI badge flights or for record flights must be sealed before the flight and unsealed afterwards by an official SSA observer. The barograph must function throughout the flight and give a continuous trace for the flight to be validated. Most barographs are very reliable, but there are many heartrending stories circulating in soaring where Diamonds have been lost due to barograph malfunctions.

When they work fine, you never hear about them. When they fail, you hear loud cries of anguish. Serious attempts on world records usually involve carrying two barographs in case one fails.

Since a barograph is a relatively simple instrument, there are a few homemade types around which seem to work fine. By far the greatest number in use today are the Winter, the Peravia, the Replogle, and the O/K. A word about each.

The O/K barograph is the latest on the market and the least expensive, selling for $90.00 It features a "feather-touch pen with anti-gel ink for permanent records on printed charts (paper)."

The Peravia is by far the most expensive and sells for over seven hundred dollars. It records on a continuous roll of paper so that many flights may be made without changing the paper. It operates by having a mechanism punch a small hole in the paper every six seconds, forming a line which is the plot of altitude vs. time. The exclusive distributor for Peravia in the United States is Mercotec Corporation of New York.

The Replogle is a simpler instrument selling for about $129. The paper must be changed after each revolution of the drum which means usually after every flight. The Replogle is made in the United States and is distributed by its designer Mr. Ed Replogle, as well as other soaring suppliers.

The Winter is made in Germany but is distributed by most United States suppliers of soaring merchandise. It sells for about $175 and can be obtained with an ink pen model that writes on graph paper, or with a stylus model that writes on a smoked aluminum foil. The smoked aluminum foil model is the most popular and is considered to be the most reliable. Inks are sometimes known to clog up or freeze at higher altitudes; and since it is imperative to get a continuous trace, not all pilots trust the ink pen model. The disadvantage of the smoked drum foil model is simply that the drum must be smoked before each use, which is usually done by holding the drum over a burning block of camphor.

Most models are available with different altitude ranges and are sometimes calibrated in feet and sometimes in meters. Unless you anticipate extremely high wave flights, it is usually better to stick with not over a 25,000 foot model so that the trace is more spread out and easy to read. Each instrument is furnished with a calibration trace when new, and additional calibration traces can be made periodically as needed to verify the accuracy of the instrument. This can be done at any good instrument shop. It is a relatively easy job to use the calibration trace with a good set of calipers to determine any absolute altitude reached and indicated on the trace.

Serious cross country and competition pilots regularly use barograph traces to make an analysis of their flights. Much can be learned from a careful scrutiny of the trace. The slope of the trace at any point is a measure of the climb or sink rate. This makes it possible to "see" from the trace what the strength of the thermals was at any time during the flight. You can also easily notice how many minutes you were in any particular thermal and how many feet of altitude were gained during that time. It is also easy to count the number of thermals used over a given time, and get a quick visual picture of what you consider the height band throughout the flight. Study of barograph traces is highly recommended as a postflight critique.

9.9 COMPUTERS

The computers referred to here are not the mighty IBM digital monsters usually associated with the name. Here we are speaking of a final glide computer which helps you make the important in-flight decision of when to start the final glide and enables you to monitor the final glide while it is underway. These computers usually consist of a simple plastic or cardboard type circular slide rule looking device. Some of them tend to be too complicated and take too much time to decipher in flight.

In general, it should be said that if the computer is not very, very simple, and if you are not intimately familiar with it, then it is doubtful that it will do you any good. It is better to make your own computer because this helps you to understand its operation.

Various manufacturers and suppliers sell computers for various sailplanes. These are rather complicated in that they are designed around the polar of a particular sailplane, and tell you exactly what speed to fly on final glide for various wind conditions. As a beginning, we recommend that you make up a simple table, perhaps with various L/Ds across the top and various altitudes down the left side. Then fill in the blocks of this table with the proper mileages. Since L/D is the slope of the glide path, it is a simple matter to figure out how many miles you can go for any given altitude. This little table can be used in lieu of a computer. You simply take the interthermaling speed that you have been flying just previous to your last thermal and for this speed value, look up (on another little table on the back of the first one which you have taken from your sailplane polar and shows the L/D for various air speeds) the L/D for the air speed you have been flying.

Knowing this L/D, then you go to the first table mentioned and with the known distance taken from your map, you can see how many feet of altitude are required to traverse this mileage. With a head wind, you should make an extra allowance by assuming a lower L/D and with a tail wind, a higher L/D. Always give yourself a little margin in altitude by planning to climb an extra several hundred feet above the minimum needed. With more experience you will be able to shave this margin down. With the help of a graphically inclined friend, you can easily transfer this table information to a straight or circular sliding scale so that you can set the scale to the L/D in question and simply read the altitude required vs. the mileage at any place on the computer.

As you progress towards your goal, you can see whether or not you are making good the L/D you assumed. This whole use of the computer should be a fast, simple, one-handed operation of only 10 or 15 seconds. This assumes, of course, that you have marked your map so that you can read mileage from your destination directly with a glance. Then another glance at the computer will be all the time needed. You just cannot afford to spend time on the computer to the extent that it interferes with your flying.

Final glide technique is an important part of the cross country soaring pilot's repertoire. It takes a great amount of practice by actually making final glides and utilization of the computer before this technique is perfected. There is no more thrilling moment in soaring than the realization at the end of a flight that you have finally "got the field made." There is hardly any more embarrassing experience than to miss the final glide and be forced to land in the field adjacent to the airport.

Fig. 9.5 is a simple glide calculator, as mentioned above, which can be made in a few minutes. If you would rather not destroy these pages in the book, then have it Xeroxed. Cut out from the book or from the Xeroxed copy, parts a and b. From the local dimestore, get a plastic self-laminating

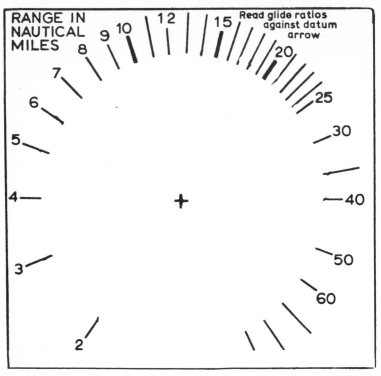

FIGURE 9.5 (a & b) GLIDE CALCULATOR (from Sailplane & Gliding; June—July 1966, page 220; article by Ian Strachan)

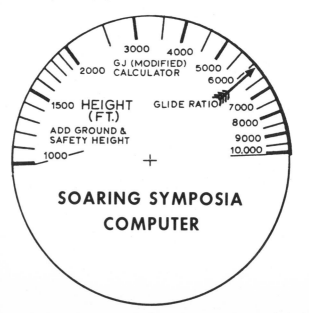

kit, which is simply a few sheets of clear plastic with sticky on one side with which you seal I.D. cards, Social Security cards, etc. Put a sheet of this on each side of each of the two parts and trim. Join the two parts together by carefully cutting or punching a small hole in the center and using a rivet or a very short 6/32 inch brass screw with a washer on either side and by brading the back after it has been tightened just enough to give the proper friction.

Notice that the range is given in nautical miles and to use this computer you should have your map marked off with circles giving nautical mile distance from you goal. It is a good idea to take an old sectional map and cut the low end of the nautical mile scale off for about 20 or 30 miles and glue it onto the side of part a before you seal it in plastic. To use the computer, simply set the glide ratio arrow of part b opposite the glide ratio of part a that you feel you can make good. Then, knowing how far you are from your goal, notice opposite this figure on part a what your required altitude must be on part b. This calculator has been simplified drastically and does not give the correct speed-to-fly for various wind conditions, etc. For more detail on the original version, you might refer to old issues of *Sailplane and Gliding,* particularly February, 1960, page 14-16, and June and July, 1966, page 220.

9.10   PERSONAL EQUIPMENT

There is no end to the list of personal equipment that could be discussed. We will limit our list to a few important items. The right type of hat is important. A white one will stay cooler and will not absorb as much heat. One with a broad, but not too broad, brim will offer the most protection from the sun for the neck as well as for the eyes. A soft hat is necessary to keep from scratching the canopy.

Good walking shoes are important, especially in the desert regions. Sneakers are OK for the populous East U.S., but be sure your shoes are comfortable enough for a few miles of walking. For cold weather flying, the Kiwi flying boots from New Zealand sold by Graham Thomson Ltd. are preferred by a great many pilots who do not want to bother with the inconvenience of batteries, wires, and the like of heated socks.

Many of the newer sailplanes have large canopies for greater visibility and oftentimes the entire upper surface area of the pilot is exposed to the direct rays of the sun throughout the flight. In such a case it certainly pays to wear extremely light colored clothing, preferably white, during the usually warmer summer months of the soaring season. The need for plenty of liquid was expressed earlier, but it should be reemphasized that high energy food of any kind is good. Nonmeltable candy, dried fruits, space sticks, etc., are preferred. In the past few years many pilots have switched from water to Gatorade.

Careful observation around a contest or active soaring center is the best lesson in what to do about personal equipment.

No chapter on soaring instruments and equipment would be complete without mention of one other small item which might be considered personal. This is the yaw string. Sometimes newcomers tend to make light of this very important instrument. The yaw string is no less important in cross country soaring than it was in training. A pilot is not totally familiar with his sailplane until he can thermal consistently without continuous reference to the yaw string. As your instructor no doubt told you in training, it is simply a much more sensitive substitute for the ball in the turn and bank. A three or four inch piece of yarn of your favorite color is usually best and can be stuck on with most any type of tape. It is worth a little trouble to be assured that it is mounted along the exact center line. Even experienced pilots who spend hundreds of hours smoothing their wings seldom complain about the drag of a yaw string to the extent that they would consider doing without it.

SAILPLANE SELECTION

10.1 INTRODUCTION

The selection of a sailplane is a very personal thing. Many factors enter into a decision on selection. In addition to the obvious factors of budget, level of experience, and personal tastes, a pilot must also decide what he is going to ask of a sailplane that he owns, before he can make a selection. Does he expect the sailplane to be extremely rugged and last a long time; does he expect the sailplane only to carry him through a Gold Badge; or, does he expect the sailplane to be the very top in competition, either in Standard or Open Class?

We will try to keep our personal opinion to ourselves in discussing the different aspects of sailplane selection, but we ask your indulgence in case an opinion or two slips in.

10.2 PERFORMANCE

The cross country soaring pilot cannot make a completely intelligent decision on sailplane selection unless he is familiar with sailplane performance and its measurement. The measuring stick for sailplane performance is the polar. This is a plot of the rate of sink vs. speed. This plot is oftentimes carried one step further and shown as a plot of L/D vs. speed. Polars may be determined from calculations even before a sailplane is built, or it is possible to actually take measurements of performance and arrive at a sailplane polar. As you would expect, the calculated polar is less reliable and is usually an optimistic forecast on the part of a designer, whereas a measured polar really tells it like it is. If you hear a salesman bragging about the outstanding polar of a sailplane, ask him if it is calculated or measured. He will probably have to admit that it is calculated, but if he does say that it is measured, ask him how and by whom.

A polar is the performance of a sailplane straight and level in stable standard air. It tells you the rate of sink or L/D at all horizontal speeds between stall and red line. The maximum L/D occurs at one speed. This is a commonly quoted figure for sailplanes and there is a great over-emphasis on this one figure. Experienced pilots are much more interested in what the L/D may be at, say 80 knots, than they are in the maximum value. When you hear competition pilots referring to and discussing the right hand side of the polar curve, this means that they are concerned about the high speed characteristics of the ship. This is referred to as penetration. The penetration of a sailplane is good if the right hand side of the polar indicates relatively high L/D's at high speeds.

It is not our intention to go into great detail in this chapter but it has been our experience that many beginners in the sport do not really understand the term L/D, or do not understand the polar. So, it might be well to spend a page or two in what we hope is a simple explanation without too much detail.

Fig. 10.1 is a sketch of a sailplane in flight at a constant air speed in smooth stable air. Naturally, the flight path is sloping downward at an angle θ because a sailplane at a constant velocity always goes down with respect to the air

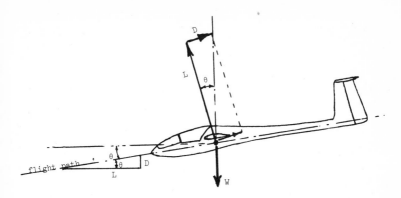

FIGURE 10.1   Tan θ = D/L $\cong$ θ
Slope of flight path = LIFT ÷ DRAG = L/D

in which it is flying. The vertical weight W must be overcome by the lift L of the wing, and this lift when added
vectorally to the drag D gives a resultant equal force opposite to the vertical weight. You can see that the little angle
θ in this triangle is the same as the angle of the glide path
and that the inverse slope of the glide path (the run over
the rise) is L/D.

In other words, the lift over drag ratio defines the glide
path of the sailplane. An L/D of 20 indicates that the
sailplane will go 20 feet forward for every foot downward.
In other words, L/D equals the glide slope; which equals
the horizontal distance divided by the vertical distance;
which equals the horizontal velocity divided by the vertical
velocity; which is also equal to the airspeed indicator
reading divided by the variometer reading (assuming no
error in the instruments).

A look at Fig. 10.2 will show a simple plot of a 1-26
polar. If we had perfectly reading instruments, we could fly
in perfectly stable, smooth air (if we could find any) and

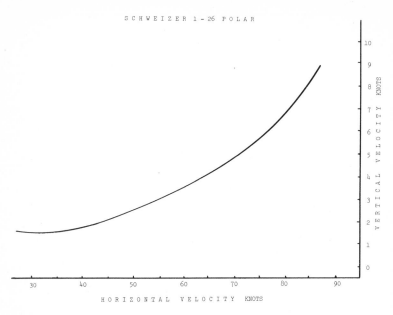

FIGURE 10.2

take readings of the variometer at various readings of the airspeed indicator and plot this horizontal velocity vs. vertical and end up with a curve like Fig. 10.2. This is a sailplane polar. However, normally, the L/D vs. horizontal velocity is plotted for this purpose.

Fig. 10.3 indicates how an L/D curve is derived from the rate of sink curve. One typical point, as an example, is taken at 65 knots. At 65 knots airspeed, we were going down 4 knots in our 1-26. If we divide these two readings, we get an L/D of 16.3 for the 1-26, at 65 knots. Using the L/D scale on the left in Fig. 10.3, we come across with a horizontal line at 16.3 L/D to 65 knots and have one point on the L/D curve. Seven other points on the L/D curve are similarly plotted, and, if you care to, you can sketch in the L/D curve through these points. You will notice

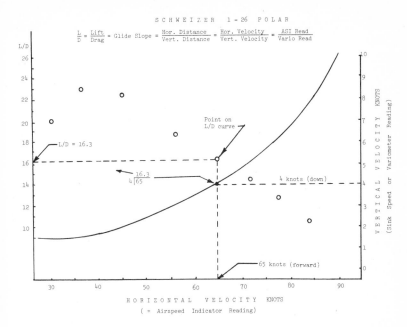

FIGURE 10.3

that the maximum L/D is about 23 and it occurs at about 40 knots.

Fig. 10.4 is a plot of the rate of sink and L/D polars for several sailplanes. Compare, for example. the Skylark 4 with the SH-Austria. The max L/D for the Skylark 4 is several points higher but the SH-1 is, in general, considered to be a better cross country sailplane. Why is this?

This example shows why the max L/D figure alone is often misleading. The fact that the max L/D for the SH-Austria occurs at 65 mph is very important. Look at the L/D for the Skylark 4 at 65 mph—or more important, look what the relative L/D's are at 75 mph. This points up the superior penetrating ability of the SH and shows why the right hand side of the polar curve is extremely important for cross country soaring.

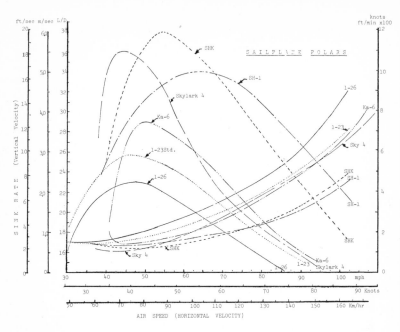

FIGURE 10.4

10.3   OTHER FLYING CRITERIA

There are many other very important flying characteristics of a sailplane besides simply its polar curve. Probably
the most important of these is the general handling qualities. How stable is the sailplane in circling flight? That is,
does it have a groovy feeling? Does it have a good roll
rate? A good sailplane should roll from 45° bank in one
direction to 45° bank in the other direction at about 1–
1½ times stall speed in about four to five seconds. It is not
hard to tell if a sailplane handles well in flight. An hour or
two in flight can settle this question. Is it easy to keep the
yaw string in the middle without a great amount of concentration? Sailplanes vary quite a bit in this respect.

FIGURE 10.5(a) Typical assembly. Trailer open, sailplane stowed inside.

Glasflügel Kestrel, as well as the Schreder HP series, are known for large roomy cockpits.

Pilot protection, in the form of a high energy absorbing

FIGURE 10.5(b)   Typical assembly. Horizontal tail assembled. Wing panels out of the trailer.

structure around the cockpit, is important in a sailplane. Schweizer pioneered this type of design in their metal sailplanes and most of the new fiberglass sailplanes meet this energy absorbing criterion.

Visibility is extremely important. It is especially true that in a sailplane you have to be able to see well to fly well.

Docility is important. In other words, what level of competence is required to fly the sailplane not only up to its peak performance, but more safely. Is it considered a

FIGURE 10.5(c)   Typical assembly. Left wing positioned and ready for right wing.

"hot" sailplane? Some high performance sailplanes are considered hot, and some of equally high performance are considered very docile.

Ruggedness and ease of maintenance are extremely important. Fiberglass and metal are superior to wood in this respect. More will be mentioned about this later.

Last, but certainly not least in the minds of many, is the ease of assembly and ground handling. If assembly requires four or five adults, a ball peen hammer, and 30 minutes of sweat, it can really take a lot of the fun out of soaring.

FIGURE 10.5(d)   Typical assembly. Wings assembled tail assembled basic assembly completed.

Many a wife will attest to the fact that it is no fun holding even a 30 pound wing tip over your head for long enduring minutes while a husband is pounding away with a hammer somewhere in the root area. The new German imports that utilize the fork and tongue wing assembly have conquered the assembly problem and most claim that assembly can be done easily with two or three persons in five minutes. Most pilots agree that the Glasflügel Standard Libelle with its 100 pound wing is about the epitome in ease of assembly and also wins the prize for the lowest wing root weight.

Landing characteristics are very important in a sailplane. Can you get it on the ground easily and safely? Are the air brakes and the wheel brake effective? Does it have a drag chute for help in landing, or does it need one? Does it have flaps for help in landing? Or does it need them?

Low speed flight characteristics are particularly important. Are the stalls gentle from all configurations and attitudes? Is there adequate stall warning? Is the spin recovery rapid and positive?

Practically all of the new sailplanes on the market today are designed to have good or excellent flight handling characteristics. This is not as much of a problem as it used to be.

10.4   GENERAL FEATURES OF IMPORTANCE

Other features of importance not directly related to performance or handling in the air are still extremely important in selecting your sailplane. Not the least of these is pilot comfort. Designers of most of the new ships are finally beginning to have pity on the pilot and have been making an effort to design comfort into the cockpits. Since it is not unusual for cross country soaring flights to last six to eight hours or even more, pilot comfort is extremely important. Most of the newer ships have semi-reclining seats which are quite nice. A few of the newer ships use the complete supine position where it appears that you are completely flat on your back. This minimizes fuselage area and helps performance. Some pilots do not like this position, but many who have the Diamants and the ASW-12's swear by the cockpit comfort of this position.

The cockpit should not only be comfortable but should be roomy. The Slingsby Skylark 4 was one of the first with a semi-reclining roomy cockpit and adequate space for extra equipment. The Schempp-Hirth Austrias and Cirruses, the

Some experienced pilots feel that the new glass ships all perform and handle about the same and, therefore, the decision to buy is based on the weight of the wing root which they must handle during assembly. Ben Greene, of North Carolina, won the 1968 U.S. National Soaring Championship in Elmira, New York, in a Libelle, using one crew man; and he claims he would not have won had he not been able to make an extremely fast retrieve and relight on the last day. The simple assembling Libelle enabled him to do this.

10.5   CONSTRUCTION TYPES

It is generally conceded that wood production sailplanes are obsolete. The American, A. J. Smith, won the standard class world championship in Poland in 1968 in a largely wooden Elfe. That was about the last of the wood breed.

There are also still a tremendous number of wood Schleicher Ka-6's and Briegleb BG-12's flying in the United States today. However, there are no sailplanes in production in the free world today that are wood and it is doubtful that we will see any more built except home built craft.

There are still many strong proponents of aluminum alloy for sailplane construction. Most notable among these are Schweizer Aircraft, Laister Aircraft, Swiss Pilatus, and Schreder's HP series.

Since the first German Phoenix flew in 1958, fiberglass laminates have grown in popularity for sailplane construction and are now well proven, generally accepted, and are probably the most popular material for high performance sailplanes. The development work took place in Germany and, to a lesser extent Switzerland, mostly during the early 60's. There are now four major producers in Germany and

FIGURE 10.6   All metal Swiss Pilatus B-4.

one in the United States using this type of construction,
and there are presently hundreds of glass sailplanes in the
United States. Proponents of fiberglass claim that a more
perfect surface can be had with less finish work, that the
material is more dimensionally stable, and that repairs can
be made more easily.

Fiberglass is generally not very stiff from a structural
standpoint and fiberglass sailplanes are known for their
weird looking large wing deflections in flight. This lack of
stiffness has been known to cause structural limitations in
some of the more exotic fiberglass designs. Newer, stiffer
materials are on the way and promise even more exciting
sailplane construction methods in the future. Graphite and
boron fibers are now available as substitutes for the glass

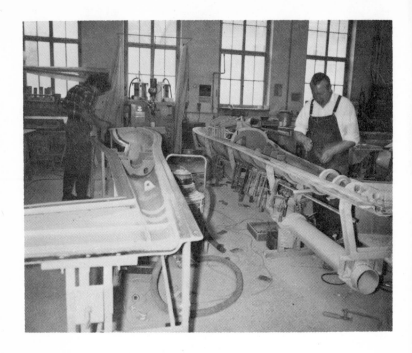

FIGURE 10.7   In a German factory.

fibers, and when their cost becomes more realistic, you can expect to see these materials used in sailplane construction.

10.6   COST VS. PERFORMANCE TRADEOFFS

The average soaring pilot who is in the market for a first cross country sailplane has a limited budget. So it is important to discuss the amount of sailplane available per dollar. This is of greater interest to many pilots than the ultimate sailplane, regardless of cost.

Starting at the bottom of the cost scale, we encounter the World War II surplus sailplanes such as the LK, Pratt-Read, TG-3, and TG-2. Except for the TG-2, which has all metal construction, these sailplanes all have wood wings, and holding that wood together are adhesives made during the war several decades ago. For this reason, we do not recommend these ships, regardless of price. Some may have been very well cared for and may still be perfectly safe.

Not counting perhaps a few off brands, we might consider next up the price list some of the older second hand Schweizers. Actually the sailplane business is not unlike the automobile business in that if we are considering resale value, it is always better to stay with the name brands. In this respect Schweizer is like Ford or Chevrolet. Their resale value is good and there is always a ready known market. We would have to say that a used 1-26 is very high on the performance per dollar scale if it is bought and sold carefully.

A little further up the performance scale is the Ka-6. Although somewhat fragile, this beautifully handling sailplane has good performance and good resale value and is definitely one of the name brands.

Very high performance open and standard class competition ships are still in short supply, and the waiting period on a new ship can vary from a few months to several years. We do not think it wise to try to give specific advice for these types ships because the market is rather tricky, to say the least, and there are also large sums of money involved in such transactions. Our best advice is to study the market as carefully as possible and talk to as many experienced pilots and owners as possible. The general statement, which should be reemphasized, is to stay with the products of well known manufacturers and beware of the one-of-a-kind sailplane.

10.7 TRAINERS

The standard beginning trainer in the United States is the Schweizer 2-33. Some schools and clubs still have the older

Schweizer 2-22, which many feel is still better for initial training. These trainers are unmatched for ruggedness and docility. The European trainers, in general, are somewhat higher performance, but are much less rugged than the Schweizers. Transition from training, all the way through cross country. has been accomplished with the 2-22, but it takes good conditions due to its marginal penetration performance. The 2-33 has much better penetration and is not an unreasonable ship to consider for tasks through the Silver C Badge. It has very effective air brakes and landing qualities which make it quite good for off-airport landings when necessary.

The only other two place ships used to any great extent for training in the United States are the Ka-7 and the

FIGURE 10.8   Schweizer 2-33

FIGURE 10.9 Blanik L-13. All metal two place import from Czechoslovakia.

ASW-13 made by the Schleicher Company of West Germany. There are a fair number of ASW-13's in the United States and a lesser number of the older model Ka-7. These ships have slightly better performance than the Schweizer and are reasonable for cross country, but they are not as rugged by our American standards.

The Blanik L-13 is a beautiful all metal trainer made in Czechoslovakia. This is almost the only trainer used in the Iron Curtain countries and well over 700 have been produced. This is a fantastic number compared to the production of any other sailplane you can name. The metal workmanship on these ships is of the highest quality and the ship is considered to be a very good trainer. There are a few in the United States, and recently the United States and

Czechoslovakia have made a reciprocity agreement on certification; there should be no licensing trouble with the Blanik even if you intend to use it as a trainer. It's still a good idea to check with your FAA-GADO office before you buy any foreign ship.

When we think of trainers, we usually think only of two place ships and dual instruction. Some transitional sailplanes can and perhaps should be thought of as trainers and the best known of these is the Schweizer 1-26. This is a rugged, docile, pleasant-to-fly little bird which is quite nice for soaring cross country on moderate tasks. A vast number of Silver C's have been completed in these ships as well as a few Gold legs and even a few Diamonds. From a training standpoint a 1-26 is a natural transition from the 2-33 and

FIGURE 10.10   Schweizer 1-26-E.

FIGURE 10.11   Schweizer 2-32.

is a nice step to take before you move up the Schweizer line to the 1-34 or 1-35. By far the vast majority of American soaring pilots began in a 2-22 or 2-33 and transitioned to the 1-26.

10.8   TWO PLACE

Most two place sailplanes are trainers of the type discussed in the previous article. There are a very few high performance two place sailplanes designed specifically for cross country and records. Discounting the several one-of-a-kinds and the common medium performance trainers mentioned in the previous article, we end up with really only one or two sailplanes to talk about. The Schweizer 2-32 is the only American sailplane of this type in production. This is an excellent cross country machine and is a beautiful thing in the air even though it handles a little heavy, as you would expect from its size. It has excellent air brakes and landing characteristics and gives no cause for concern in off-field landings. After you get it on the ground, then it's a different story. Be sure you know what you are doing before you volunteer to crew for a 2-32 pilot. Compared to single place sailplanes, this bird takes a little doing to get apart and on the trailer. It is generally true, of course, that all two place are heavier and disassembly and assembly are more of a problem than you would expect with a single place.

The Caproni A-21 represents a new class of very high performance two place fiberglass sailplane. It is in limited production, and while not inexpensive, it is the ultimate in two place sailplanes today. For those who may be inclined toward a powered glider, it comes with a small jet engine in the A-21J version.

The Schempp-Hirth Company representative displayed a drawing at the U.S. Nationals in Marfa in 1969 and at Soaring Symposia's meeting in Morgantown in 1973, to get the reaction and sample the market. This big bird, called the Janus, looked like a super two place Cirrus (Tandem seating) and caused quite a lot of talk. The reaction was generally good and we should be seeing them in the United States soon.

Perhaps another word should be mentioned here about World War II military surplus two place sailplanes. Most of these were designed to be high performance in their day but were used by the military as trainers. Except for possibly a TG-2 in good condition, we could not recommend them for reasons mentioned earlier.

10.9   POWERED SAILPLANES

In recent years powered sailplanes have gained tremendously in popularity. A power sailplane is simply a sailplane which has a small engine to take the place of the tow plane. Ordinarily the engine is shut down in flight and soaring is done in the conventional manner. It is possible, of course, to start the engine to prevent an off-airport landing, if desired.

In some cases the engine is retracted into the fuselage to minimize drag. In other cases, the propeller can be fully feathered for the same reason.

Many pilots demand the utmost in performance and those who are more competition minded are not interested in sacrificing performance by adding the complexity and weight of an engine. Proponents of the powered sailplane feel that having a means for getting aloft without the help of others greatly increases the utilization of their machine and, therefore, the fun of soaring.

The ex-editor of *Soaring* magazine, Bennett Rogers, is one of the best known and most avid proponents of powered sailplanes, or motor gliders as they are sometimes called. He sets forth the case for the powered sailplane quite well in the October, 1969 issue of *Soaring,* and anyone interested in this type of machine should read his article.

Most of the powered sailplanes in production today are made in Germany and are being imported into the United States in increasing numbers. They are also becoming very popular in Europe, and as a consequence, there appears to be several more advanced designed, higher performance motor gliders on the way. The most popular in present production are discussed below.

The Fournier RF-4D is a single place, low wing machine with engine fixed in front and a power off max glide ratio of about 20 to 1. The RF-5 model is a similar tandem two place ship. The U.S. distributor is Sport Aviation, Inc., Wooster, Ohio.

The Scheibe Company of West Germany makes three models. The SF-25C is two place, side by side seating. The SF-27M is higher performance, single place with a small engine that can be folded inside. The Tandem Falke is a tandem two place with electric starter and a feathering propeller. These are distributed in the United States by Graham Thompson Ltd., of Santa Monica, California.

The Schleicher Company, also of Germany, has available the low wing AS-K 14 which utilizes many Ka-6E parts and has a fixed engine in front. They also make a two place side by side model AS-K 16. The Schleicher distributor in the U.S. is Mr. Rudy Mozer of Bloomfield Hills, Michigan.

FIGURE 10.12   Schleicher AS-K14.

10.10 MODERN AMERICAN TYPES

After several years of dominance by the European high performance sailplanes, the American manufacturers are returning to the competition circuit with some very promising designs.

The late Art Zimmerman's Concept 70 is the first U.S. production fiberglass bird. It reflects the meticulous workmanship for which Art was famous. The Concept 70 is now beginning its contest career.

The Laister "Nugget" is another promising U.S. sailplane produced by Jack Laister who designed the LP-49 and was co-designer of the LK-10A. It features a metal wing which achieves an excellent profile by using metal to metal bond-

FIGURE 10.13 Schweizer 1-34.

ing techniques such as is used in jet aircraft. The prepro-
duction airplane has been flown in the 1971 and '73
Standard Class National contests and was completing its
certification program in mid 1973.

After a lapse of many years Schweizer Aircraft is now
producing a sailplane with championship potential. The
1-35 was first announced with a large model at the "Symposium for Competitive Soaring" in Feb. 1973 and the
prototype flew alongside the contestants at the Elmira
Regional Contest that summer. It has the largest variable
wing loading of any modern sailplane. Three hundred
twenty pounds of water ballast and a low empty weight
gives it a minimum wing loading of 5.5 lbs/ft^2 and maximum of 8.7 lbs/ft^2.

FIGURE 10.14   Schweizer 1-35.

All of these new American sailplanes use flaps rather than spoilers for glide path control as most of our designers believe the slow landing and steep approaches of flapped winged sailplanes offer the pilot a much safer approach and landing. They are also equipped to carry water ballast as are most modern competition gliders. The Laister LP-49, a Standard Class ship, which features a metal wing combined with a fiberglass fuselage can can be bought either complete or as a kit. Other American ships available in kit form are the high performance Schreder HP-Series all metal sailplanes, the Gehrlein 15-meter GP-1 all metal ship, and the Open Class BG-12-BD, which is of wood construction and is also designed for the home builder.

The LP-49 is type certified and may be licensed in the normal category, whereas the HP-14, GP-1, and BG-12-BD are licensable in the experimental category.

10.11 IMPORTS

The largest number of high performance sailplanes designed specifically for cross country and competition are the "glass birds" from Germany. We will mention each of the ships available and try to point out an outstanding feature of each.

This is a rather touchy subject so we will proceed in alphabetical order of the name of the manufacturers.

We will start with "B" for Bolkow even though this ship is no longer in production and is not available new. The Bolkow Phoebus B is a Standard Class machine and the Phoebus C is Open Class. This T-tail glass ship has many satisfied owners in the United States.

The Diamant is another T-tail beauty that was made in Switzerland by Flug & Fahrzeugwerke A.G. (F.F.A.). This machine features a fully supine pilot position which its

FIGURE 10.15   Glasflugal Standard Libelle.   (Photo by Alex Aldott)

owners claim to be very comfortable. A Diamant won the U.S. Nationals in 1970. It is also out of production.

The Glasflügel Company of West Germany makes two glass ships which are distributed in the United States by Graham Thomson Ltd., of Santa Monica, California. One is the 17-meter Kestrel and the other is the Standard Libelle. A special 22-meter Kestrel (Model 604) is also available on special order. The T-tail 17-meter Kestrel features a drag chute, air brakes, landing flaps for off-field landings and water ballast for high penetration. This ship won the German Nationals in 1969. The Libelle has a conventional tail, retractable landing gear, provisions for water ballast, but does not have a drag chute or flaps because they were not

allowable in Standard Class at the time of its design. There
are many Open Libelles (Model 301) in the United States
which do have chutes and flaps, but Glasflügel no longer
makes the Open Libelle. An Open Libelle won the U.S.
Nationals in 1968 and a Standard Libelle won the Open
Nationals in 1972. Slingsby Aircraft Company of England
makes (19-meter span) Kestrels in England, under license.

The other non-German import is the new Tee-tail standard
class PIK-20 from Finalnd. It was first flown in major competition in Australia in 1974. Its performance is reputed to be
equal to the other glass standard class ships mentioned.

Schempp-Hirth of West Germany makes the Open Class
Nimbus II and the Standard Cirrus (both T-tail). These ships

FIGURE 10.16   Kestrel 19.

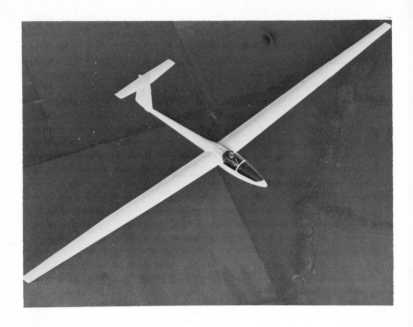

FIGURE 10.17　Kestrel 19.

are noted for their large roomy cockpits. The Open Class Nimbus won the World Soaring Championship in Yugoslavia in 1972. The Nimbus & The Standard Cirrus have provision for water ballast and the Nimbus has a drag chute. These two sailplanes, as well as the Open Cirrus (also a World Champion), were designed by Klaus Holighaus, who also built the one-of-a-kind 23-meter Nimbus (prototype of the Nimbus II) at Schempp-Hirth. This ship won the World Soaring Championship in Marfa, Texas in 1970, piloted by George Moffat. George also won the 1974 World Open Class Championship in Australia flying a Nimbus II. Rainco, of Phoenix, Arizona, is the United States' distributor for Schempp-Hirth.

The Schleicher Company, also of West Germany, makes two high performance glass birds in addition to their two

FIGURE 10.18 **Schempp-Hirth Standard Cirrus.**

place and motor gliders. One is the Standard Class ASW-15B with a conventional tail and the other is the ASW-17. The ASW-17 is reputed to have the best performance at 100 knots of any sailplane in production today. It utilizes flaps and air brakes for landing but does not have a drag chute. Both of these have provision for water ballast. George Moffat also won the U.S. National Open Championship in 1973 at Liberal, Kansas, flying an ASW-17. Schleicher sailplanes are distributed in the United States by Mr. Rudy Mozer of Bloomfield Hills, Michigan.

The Schneider Company of West Germany makes the Standard Class T-tail LS-1. This sailplane has an excellent reputation in Germany and is in great demand. As a consequence, it has been slow in reaching the United States, with delivery time reported to be quite long. The LS-1 won the Standard Class World Championship in 1970.

A comment or two about all of these glass birds. Most utilize the tongue and fork wing assembly scheme which seems to be standard in Europe now, and this makes them all relatively easy to assemble although the wing weight of the Diamant, Nimbus, 604, and ASW-17 makes them a handful for two people, and very difficult for one female on the wing tip. The top level Standard Class are all quite close in performance and most other aspects in that they all handle quite well and the weight of the 15 meter wings make them quite reasonable to assemble with only one person besides the pilot for a crew.

How much do these glass birds cost? The Standard Class ships are all 25,000 to 30,000 DM, and with the present

FIGURE 10.19   Schempp-Hirth Nimbus II.

exchange rate this means $7500 to $10,000 ex-works, at the factory, without trailer or instruments. This means you must add about $2000 to $2500 for a trailer, another $1500 for instruments, another $400 or $500 for shipping and insurance, and another $400 or $500 for U.S. duty. Between $12,000 and $15,000 is not too far off for the complete package, however, it is always possible to save a little money by building your own trailer and perhaps using a minimum of instruments, etc. Open Class ships vary a little more but are around $15,000 plus the extras, which puts them in the $18,000 to $25,000 class for the complete package. Generally speaking, used fiberglass sailplanes are selling at a premium in the United States today and bargains are hard to find. For example, it is not unusual to pay over $10,000 for an Open Libelle complete with trailer and instruments, ready to go and in excellent condition.

In general, these imported fiberglass ships are all very well designed, rate very high in performance, are very rugged and are easy to repair. All generally have excellent handling qualities, and are easy to assemble and handle on the ground. The only way to store one of these precision machines is in an enclosed trailer and in bad weather and in the winter, most owners even keep the trailers inside.

10.12   SUMMARY

When selecting a sailplane, you should not only consider one that is within your budget but, more important, you should consider one that is within your experience range. A fat checkbook cannot buy experience. Buying a supership does not make you a superpilot. A really superpilot is super-careful with his supership and we should remember that a supership can make a supernut superdead superquick. Seriously, it is a well known fact that too many accidents in recent years have resulted from an over-enthusastic pilot with limited experience, buying a low drag, high wing loading sailplane, and over-extending his capabilities.

Treat these new slippery birds with the respect they demand and keep the fun and safety in cross country soaring.

FAA—FAR—FAI

11.1 INTRODUCTION

The total number of airplanes in the U.S. is outnumbered by the people who work for the agency which controls all facets of aviation. The Federal Air Regulations (F.A.R.) are the laws of this great bureau and govern all of us who are associated in any way with aircraft. Those who work every day with these rules and regulations are the people of the Federal Aviation Administration (FAA). They are often frustrated by the rules just as we are when we complain about the rationality of certain portions of them. So, by working with the people of the FAA, you will be able to fly sooner and more often with fewer aggravating frustrations.

As we go through these tips, keep in mind that these rules are law; but they are administered by people so try to get along with the people as well as abiding by the rules.

11.2 SAILPLANE LICENSES

A sailplane is licensed and airworthy in a legal sense when these three official papers are carried in the airplane:
  1. An Aircraft Registration properly made out and showing the true owner of the sailplane.

2. An Airworthiness Certificate which states that the aircraft was inspected when manufactured and pronounced airworthy at that time.

3. A log book completed to date and showing that the aircraft has been inspected within the past 12 months by an authorized mechanic and bearing his statement and signature to this effect.

The aircraft's registration is not a bill of sale and does not show any liens that may be held against the ship. The bill of sale is a separate form and does not need to be carried in the sailplane.

If you are importing a sailplane, the FAA airworthiness certificate will not accompany it when it arrives. You or your agent, or dealer, must have it inspected by an FAA maintenance or engineering inspector after it has cleared customs and been delivered. This inspector must be shown the foreign equivalent of the airworthiness certificate which must match in make and model the proper FAA specification sheet that will be the basis of its U.S. standard type certificate. This is one of those times to remember that the inspector is a human being who has a rather difficult job, for these papers must match or he cannot issue the aircraft registration. So the wisest thing is to visit your local FAA general aviation district office (G.A.D.O,) and tell them you are importing a sailplane and ask their help well in advance of the time your ship arrives. A call to them before you purchase the sailplane is a wise precaution. Some foreign sailplanes are difficult to license through normal channels in the U.S.

Notice the term *standard* type certificate. The other class is the *experimental* type certificate. The experimental type certificate is issued to sailplanes that do not comply with the manufacturing regulations of the FAR. Maybe they are

The United States of America
DEPARTMENT OF TRANSPORTATION
Federal Aviation Administration

GLIDER

Type Certificate

IMPORT

Number G12EU

This certificate, issued to GLASFLUGEL Company , Schlattstall, Federal Republic of Germany certifies that the type design for the following product with the operating limitations and conditions therefor as specified in the Civil Air Regulations and the Type Certificate Data Sheet, meets the airworthiness requirements of Part 21.29 of the Federal Aviation Regulations.

H 301 "Libelle"

This certificate, and the Type Certificate Data Sheet which is a part hereof, shall remain in effect until surrendered, suspended, revoked, or a termination date is otherwise established by the Administrator of the Federal Aviation Administration.

Date of application: November 4, 1964

Date of issuance: May 31, 1967

By direction of the Administrator

(Signature) for Walter R. Haldeman

(Title) Chief, Aircraft Certification Staff
Europe, Africa, and Middle East Region

This certificate may be transferred if endorsed as provided on the reverse hereof.

Any alteration of this certificate and/or the Type Certificate Data Sheet is punishable by a fine of not exceeding $1,000, or imprisonment not exceeding 3 years, or both.

Form FAA-381 (3-59)

FIGURE 11.1

home built, or the manufacturer has not completed the airworthiness certification process, or in the case of certain foreign makes, the country may not have an agreement with the U.S. concerning the exchange of licensing rights.

Regardless of the reason, these simple rules apply to experimental aircraft. The annual inspection cannot be done by a designated aircraft mechanic, but must be accomplished by an FAA inspector. An experimental aircraft must be inspected each time it is sold. However, you can work on it yourself and any modifications you make do not affect its airworthiness papers as long as you inform the FAA inspector about any major mod's. You cannot carry passengers or goods for hire in an experimental ship; but since most gliders are single place, this only means you can't rent them.

Standard Type Certificates mean you can rent, and your local designated mechanic can do the annual inspections. However, you cannot modify it in any way. A periodic or annual inspection differs from a 100 hour check only in paper work.

Tips about inspections: Ask the agent or mechanic if it is okay for you to remove the inspection covers and prepare it for inspection. He will usually give his enthusiastic approval for this is sometimes the most time-consuming portion of a routine inspection.

Don't ask him to approve of your latest installation of a radio, or barograph case, or a battery, etc. These are items that affect the airworthiness of the sailplane and the work should be done by a licensed mechanic or done under his supervision and signed off as airworthy by a licensed mechanic *before* the inspection begins.

Have all your papers available, with your aircraft log book up to date.

Don't ask the inspector, or inspecting mechanic, to approve of anything that is not in his opinion airworthy. Don't argue with him, remember his livelihood depends on his mechanic's license; and he can lose it if he breaks the law, which is the FAR. Keep in mind this advice: People in bureaus are often frustrated, too, so don't aggravate their frustrations. They also know the regulations and are kept informed by newsletters of chronic problems of various types of aircraft, including sailplanes. Perhaps the criticisms of your work may stem from a letter from Washington telling them of an accident caused by the very thing you are pressing him to accept.

11.3   FLIGHT TESTS

Since we presume you are new at soaring, perhaps you have not taken your Private flight test and are preparing to pass this while you are becoming proficient in soaring cross country. FAA Booklet AC-61-43 "Glider Written Exam. Guide" shows the way to prepare for the written, and we shall take up some tips on passing the flight test.

The flight examiner wants to discover two things through the medium of the flight test. First, are you proficient and knowledgeable and, second, does your judgment qualify you for your rating? He can determine your ability to fly the sailplane by watching your airspeed control and the smooth way you complete the required maneuvers. But you must think and speak for him to qualify your judgment. Tell him what you are doing. Tell him what you are thinking. If you have forgotton the sequence of the maneuvers he gave you earlier, ask him. He's human and he will realize you are a bit nervous about the test.

Sailplane flying requires precise airspeed control. The examiner will watch this very closely. Landing away requires planning, therefore, the examiner will carefully evaluate your pattern flying. He will also be very interested in your spot landing for the same reason.

Just stay cool and take him for a nice ride complete with a few comments.

11.4   INTERPRETATION OF THE FAR

Just as all laws are interpreted to achieve their full meaning, the Federal Air Regulations require study and some translation. For instance:

INSTRUMENT FLYING IN SAILPLANE. Soon after we have soloed and successfully thermaled to the base of a cloud, we begin to wonder about continuing our climb up into the cloud itself. With proper training and a well equipped ship, this is a feasible next step for the advanced soaring pilot *except* for the FAR.

Since flight within the control area is prohibited without clearance from airway traffic control and nearly all the eastern U.S. airspace is now within control areas, instrument flight in the eastern U.S. in a sailplane is effectively prohibited.

Should you possess an instrument rating and your sailplane is properly equipped, you can fly into the clouds as long as you are in those remote regions where you are clear of the control areas or you have obtained ATC clearance.

Instrument flight is also limited to below 18,000 feet for above that altitude air traffic is controlled throughout the U.S.

In designated mountain wave areas such as Sugarbush, Vermont, and Colorado Springs, special arrangements have been made with ATC to allow clearance above the 18,000 foot limit during times agreed to by prior arrangements.

The real fact is that all soaring flight in clouds within the U.S. has almost become illegal. Flight through control zones should not be made without radio contact with the tower because it is just not very smart. The beauty of soaring is in the sense of freedom one enjoys while flying so why not stay away from these hubs of aerial commerce and enjoy your freedom.

The FAR says gliders have priority over powered planes in landing. The use of this priority is a very dangerous presumption and besides the soaring clubs have enough problems without aggravating the power pilots and the airport management by the exercise of your prior rights in a glider.

To sum up, stay clear of all clouds and avoid areas of heavy traffic.

11.5   THE FAI

Enough with Federal Bureaus, let us now consider the sport of soaring and the attendant badges and associated records.

The Federation Aeronautique International (FAI) is the international organization that records all aviation events of note and the committee on soaring of that body is known by its initials, the CIVV. The National Aeronautical Association is the official United States representative of the FAI and the Soaring Society of America has been delegated as its authority on soaring matters in the U.S. OSTIV is a volunteer technical committee of the CIVV which meets every two years to accept technical papers of interest to soaring. The publication of these papers may be obtained through the SSA. These are printed in the language presented, however, and it is usually several months after the meeting before they are published.

Soaring rules such as the badge requirements are those of the FAI as set by the CIVV administered in the U.S. by the SSA as delegated by the NAA.

The Gold and Diamond distance tasks may be completed in as many as three legs as long as the two turnpoints are properly declared before takeoff (see Fig. 11.2), and proof is submitted of passing these turnpoints when claiming the badge legs.

An interesting difference in the FAI rules deletes the 28 percent rule for badge flights. The Diamond Goal flight must be a goal and return or a completed triangle task. Since the length of the shortest leg is not a factor, laying out the triangle can be interesting as shown in Fig. 11.3. This proposed flight can also qualify for the Gold Distance. Declaration for this example is shown in Fig. 11.2.

The pilot in this example has chosen to use the ridges to achieve his Goal Diamond and Gold Distance. The south turnpoint is well marked by the winding highway crossing the ridge 49.5 miles from Newcastle, his takeoff point and declared goal. The northern turnpoint is the pass—47 miles northeast marked by the railroad, river, and highway traversing a narrow ravine. The total distance flown will be at least twice the length of each leg or 193 miles but the distance claimed must be 191.5 as only two turnpoints can be declared (49.5 + 47 + 95 = 191.5).

This task is to be flown as a combination of two goal and return legs to complete a Diamond Goal and Gold distance with maximum retrieve of no more than 50 miles airline distance. An extension of this principle makes a Diamond Distance possible with two 80 mile legs, one up the ridge and one down the ridge for a total of 320 miles.

According to Rule 7.3.4 "Gold or Diamond Distance may be claimed from an uncompleted triangle provided that 300, or 500 km, or more is flown and the glider is landed not more than 10 km off the line of the last leg." If you were attempting a Diamond Goal flight and landed slightly short, it is possible to get credit for Gold distance

FLIGHT DECLARATION

DATE SEPT. 4 1973 **TIME** 9:20 E.D.T.

I HEREBY DECLARE THE FOLLOWING FLIGHT ATTEMPT

Departure Point NEWCASTLE

Lat. 37°-28'N.   **Long.** 80°-06'W.

TURNPOINTS:

First HIGHWAY HAIRPIN TURN

Lat. 37°-08'N   **Long.** 80°-54'W

Second RAILROAD-RIVER-HIGHWAY

Lat. 38°-00'-30"N   **Long.** 79°-33'W

GOAL: NEWCASTLE

Lat. 37°-28'N   **Long.** 80°-06'W

Sailplane SCHWEIZER 1-26 N8226R

(MAKE, MODEL, REG. NO.)

PILOT JAMES Mc DOE

(PRINT)

Signature James Mc Doe

I hereby certify the above to be a proper flight declaration made in my presence at time above.

SSA Official
Observer: WILLIAM C. HOLBROOK

(PRINT)

Signature William C. Holbrook

GOLD "C" #197

SSA ITEM No.80

FIGURE 11.2

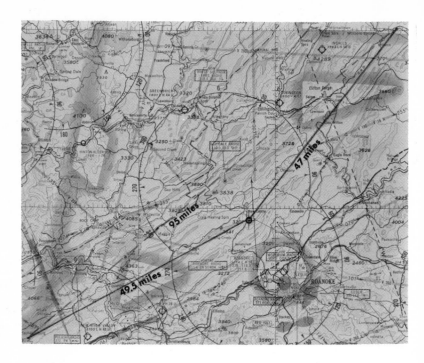

FIGURE 11.3   Diamond goal and gold distance triangle.

if your total allowed distance was 300 km. The Diamond
would not be credited unless you made your goal.

The 28 percent rule still applies on record attempts
(state, national, and world). This rule states that the shortest leg of a triangle must be more than 28 percent of the
total distance *claimed* for the flight to qualify under the
FAI Sporting Code rules. For example, the minimum length
of the shortest leg of a 192 mile flight being used for a 300
km (186.42 miles) badge is 53.76 miles which is 28% of
192 and not 28% of 186.42.

The ratio of height to distance flown cannot be ignored
especially under the new rules. When the difference in

FAI SPORTING CODE
RULE 2.1.7

The distance penalty on a 62.2 mile (100 Km) flight shall be 40 times the height loss over 3,281 feet (1000 meters).

Example:

62.2 mile flight
4000 feet M.S.L. release altitude
Sea level landing altitude

$$
\begin{array}{rl}
4000 & \text{feet} \\
-\ \ 3281 & \text{feet allowable loss} \\
\hline
719 & \text{excess altitude loss} \\
\times\ \ \ 40 & \\
\hline
28{,}760 & \text{feet} - \text{penalty}
\end{array}
$$

$$
\begin{array}{rl}
28{,}760 & = 5.45 \text{ miles} \\
62.14 & \text{miles flown} \\
-\ \ 5.45 & \text{penalty} \\
\hline
56.69 & \text{allowable distance}
\end{array}
$$

Figure 11.4

altitude between the landing point and the release altitude exceeds one percent of the distance flown on flights of 62.2 miles (100 km) or less, a penalty of 40 times the excess is subtracted from the total distance flown. The maximum altitude difference allowed on flights over 62.2 miles is 3281 feet (1000 meters). A height loss greater than this results in the same 40 to 1 subtraction from the distance flown.

Figure 11.4 is the calculation of the penalty when the landing point on a 62.2 mile flight was only 719 feet lower than the allowable altitude loss; 5.45 miles penalty is well over 8½ percent of the total distance. This could be a heartbreaker on a Gold Distance flight of 190 miles, for the penalty of releasing 719 feet too high would subtract enough mileage to reduce the distance allowed to below 186.42 mile requirement.

So on planning your Silver "C" attempt, your landing point must be less than 1642 feet below your *release* altitude on a 31.1 mile flight, or 2112 feet on a 40 mile flight. The simplest solution is to plan a 40 mile flight and release 2000 feet higher than your goal.

The Soaring Society of America, Inc.
Box 66071, Los Angeles, Calif. 90066

SSA Item #39 — STATE SOARING RECORDS RULES & APPLICATION FORM

1. Classification and Definition of Records
   1.1 Classification of Records - The classes of records shall be as follows:
      1. Open
         a. Single-Place
         b. Multi-Place

      2. Senior
         a. Single-Place
         b. Multi-Place
      3. Junior
         a. Single-Place
         b. Multi-Place
      For each of these classes, the following records are recognized:
      a) Distance - distance in a straight line.
      b) Goal - distance in a straight line to a goal.
      c) Out and Return - distance in a straight line to a predesignated turn point
         and return to the point of departure.
      d) Gain of Altitude.
      e) Absolute Altitude.
      f) Speed over a triangular course of 100 km. (62.14 mi.)
      g) Speed over a triangular course of 200 km. (124.28 mi.)
      h) Speed over a triangular course of 300 km. (186.42 mi.)
      i) Speed over a triangular course of 500 km. (310.70 mi.)
   1.2 State Records must comply with the FAI rules for National and International Records.
      Exceptions will be made as listed in Section 2 of these regulations unless the
      record exceeds a National or International Record. (Note: The FAI rules specify,
      among other things; that the flight must exceed the previous record by 6.214 mi.
      for records measured by distance, by 3% for altitude records, and by 1.24 mph for
      speed records; and speed starts may not be more than 3281 ft. above the ground.)
   1.3 The record flight must originate within the state. (Note: There is no require-
      ment that the pilot or passenger must be residents of the state.)
   1.4 Senior Class. The pilot, and passengers (in the multi-place sub-class), must be
      of an experience level less than Gold C. When a Senior Record exceeds a record
      for the Open Class, it will be listed in the Open Record list and in the Senior
      Record list.
   1.5 Junior Class. The pilot, and passengers (in the multi-place sub-class), must be
      under 21 years of age. When a Junior Record exceeds a record in the Senior and/or
      Open Class, it will be entered in the Senior and/or Open Record list and in the
      Junior Record list.
   1.6 All National and International record flights originating in the state and recog-
      nized by the SSA, NAA, and FAI will automatically be registered as State Records
      without application.
   1.7 Former National or International Records (not in effect on July 1, 1958) origi-
      nating in the state may be certified as State Records if application is made
      before January 1, 1959.
   1.8 Applications for records (other than National or International Records) must be
      made on the official application form within 30 days of the flight to the Chairman
      of the State Record Homologation Committee but the Chairman must be notified
      within 10 days after the flight in writing. The Chairman will be appointed by
      the SSA State Governor.

2. General Regulations and Definitions
   2.1 The pilot in command must be a voting member or Student Member of SSA.
   2.2 All record attempts must be conducted within the Federal Aviation Regulations.
   2.3 An application for a record will not be accepted if during the flight an accident occurred which rendered the aircraft unairworthy or injuries were sustained by the pilot or crew that required hospitalization.
   2.4 More than one record may be claimed for a single flight.
   2.5 Measures of altitude will be in feet, distance in miles, and speed in miles per hour.
   2.6 All record attempts must be witnessed at take-off, turning points, and landing by an SSA Official Observer (a Member of SSA who holds at least a C badge). Exceptions will be made for landings after a distance flight or goal flight (not out and return) if two responsible persons sign as witnesses, and for turning points on an out-and-return or speed flight if two responsible persons sign as witnesses or if photographic evidence of a quality acceptable to FAI and certified to by an SSA Official Observer is submitted.
   2.7 All applications for records must be accompanied by a barogram calibrated by an SSA Official Observer. Exceptions will be made if the barogram is on file with the SSA for the awarding of an FAI Badge. The barograph must have been sealed by the SSA Official Observer and the seal broken by the Observer. (Note: Continual observation will not substitute for a barogram.)
   2.8 Record attempts by powered gliders will be accepted if the stoppage of the engine is discernible on the barogram and if the engine is not operated again in flight. A witness must attest to where the glider was when the engine stopped.
   2.9 Launching may be made by any method but should be indicated on the barogram by a small loss of altitude immediately after release. For distance flights less than 62.2 mi., the loss of altitude between the point of release and the point of landing must not exceed 1% of the distance covered. When the loss of altitude is more than 3281 feet, the distance certified shall be the true distance covered less 30 times the loss of height reduced by 3281 feet.
   2.10 In the case of goal or out-and-return flights, one goal (geographical coordinates or a landmark or an airport) must be stated in written form immediately prior to the flight and the pilot's signature witnessed by an SSA Official Observer. The landing must be made within 3281 feet of the designated landing point.
   2.11 For gain of altitude record, the altitude certified is the difference between the greatest altitude registered on the barogram and the lowest altitude previously registered after release.
   2.12 Absolute altitude records must have a gain in altitude of at least 3281 ft.
   2.13 Speed flights will be timed from the time that the glider crosses the starting plane until the glider crosses the finish plane at the end of the flight. These flights must be timed by an SSA Official Observer.
   2.14 The triangular courses for speed courses must measure at least the distance of the record course being flown (100, 200, 300 or 500 km.) and less than the next longer course length. No side of the triangle may be less than 28% of the total course length flown. The (no more than) two turn points must be stated in written form immediately prior to the flight and the pilot's signature witnessed by an SSA Official Observer.

- 3 -

3. Record Application Form (Submit one copy)

Date of Application_____

3.1 General Information
1. First Pilot's Full Name_____
   First Pilot's Address_____
   FAA Pilot Certificate (Ratings and Serial No.)_____
   Juniors only - Date of Birth_____ For Open Class Pilots: Date of flight
2. Passenger's Full Name_____ that completed Gold Badge_____
   Passenger's Address_____
   Weight plus Chute plus Ballast (must be at least 165 lbs.)_____
   Juniors only - Date of Birth_____
3. Record(s) applied for: State_____
   Class 1. Open - Single-place_____ 4. Senior - Multi-place_____
         2. Open - Multi-place_____ 5. Junior - Single-place_____
         3. Senior - Single-place_____ 6. Junior - Multi-place_____
   Record a. Distance_____ e. Absolute Altitude_____ i. Speed-
          b. Goal_____ f. Speed - 100 km._____   500 km.____
          c. Out and Return____ g. Speed - 200 km._____
          d. Gain of Altitude___ h. Speed - 300 km._____
4. Point of Departure (Release point) Latitude_____Longitude_____
   Date of Flight_____ Distance claimed _____ miles
   Sailplane (Make and Model)_____
   FAA Registration No._____ Altitude claimed _____ feet
3.2 Barogram. Enclosed_____. Filed with SSA_____. Gain claimed_____ ft.
   Method of Launch
   From Barogram Altitude of Take-off ASL:_____
                  Altitude of Release ASL:_____
                  Low point after release ASL:_____
                  High point of flight ASL:_____
                  High point after lowpoint after release ASL:_____
                  Altitude of landing ASL:_____

Calibrated by_____
                    SSA Official Observer

3.3 Goal Flights or Out-and-Return Flights or Speed Flights. Written declaration
    of goal or turning point(s) must be attached and signed by Pilot and SSA Official.
3.4 Out-and- Return or Speed Flights. Evidence of passing over turning point(s) must
    be attached (signed statement of one SSA Official Observer or signed statement of
    two witnesses or photographic evidence attested to by an SSA Official Observer).
3.5 Speed Flights only: Distance around triangle,_____ miles
    Take-off time_____ Time at starting plane_____
    Release time_____ Time at finish plane _____
    Landing time_____ Speed claimed _____

                        Signature of SSA
                        Official Observer _____

- 4 -

3.6 Certificate of Landing - Location_____ Lat._____ Long._____
        Date _____ Time_____
                        SSA Official Observer _____
                (If not SSA Official Observer state profession)_____
                        Second Witness_____
                        Address_____

Note: Signatures for Items 3.3, 3.4, 3.6 may be omitted if flight is on file with SSA
       for an FAI Badge.

3.7 General Description of Flight by Pilot (at least 100 words)

We certify to the best of our knowledge that the above is true:

        Pilot's Signature   _____

        Passenger's Signature   _____

        SSA Official Observer   _____

        Date form received by record keeper _____

        Approved by   _____
                                    (signature of record keeper)
        Date approved_____

        Date record certificate issued _____

INDEX

ABOUT THE AUTHORS

ED BYARS:

Started soaring in 1956 in University of Illinois Club while in graduate school. Received his Silver C, Commercial Glider rating, as well as a Ph.D. in Engineering while there. Holds Diamond Badge No, 102. Has about a thousand glider hours as well as several thousand power. Soloed power in 1945 and presently flies IFR Bonanza for business and pleasure. Flies Open Class Glasflügel Kestrel sailplane in competition and cross country. Competes in Nationals and eastern regionals regularly. Has written various articles for *Soaring* and *Sailplane and Gliding* in recent years. Is presently Professor and Chairman of Department of Mechanical Engineering and Mechanics of West Virginia University at Morgantown, West Virginia.

BILL HOLBROOK:

Started soaring in 1958 when he helped form the Cumberland Soaring Group. Holds Diamond Badge No. 251. Started flying in military in 1942 and flew PBY's during the war for the Army. Has ATR with various ratings. Is Chief Pilot and Director of Flight Operations for Kelly Springfield Tire Company in Cumberland, Maryland, flying Lear jets and prop jets. Bill is the driving force behind the Cumberland Soaring Group - owning and maintaining the PA-18 tow plane and acting as designated FAA Examiner (glider). Built from scratch an Open Class HP 13:5 sailplane and now flies a 301-B Libelle in competition and cross country. Holds world out and return record with a 783 mile ridge flight. Longest soaring flight ever made in United States. Longest flight by an American. Second longest flight in world. Competes in U.S. Nationals and eastern regionals regularly. Won the Smirnoff Transcontinental Sailplane Derby Race.

GOLDEN EAGLE 1

Span 45' Length 21'
Max. Chord 50" Heig
Wing Area 155 sq. f
Weight 310 lbs.
Asp. Ratio 13.4
Wing Section G535-C
Min. sink 55"/sec.

SCHNEIDER   BOOMERANG